PRAISE FOR THE PLAYS OF NEIL LABUTE

THE MERCY SEAT

"[A] powerful drama . . . LaBute shows a true master's hand in guiding us amid the shoals and reefs of a mined relationship."
—Donald Lyons, *New York Post*

"Though set in the cold, gray light of morning in a downtown loft with inescapable views of the vacuum left by the twin towers, *The Mercy Seat* really occurs in one of those feverish nights of the soul in which men and women lock in vicious sexual combat, as in Strindberg's *Dance of Death* and Edward Albee's *Who's Afraid of Virginia Woolf?*"   —Ben Brantley, *The New York Times*

"An intelligent and thought-provoking drama that casts a less-than-glowing light on man's dark side in the face of disaster . . . The play's energy lies in LaBute's trademark scathing dialogue."
—Robert Dominguez, *Daily News*

THE SHAPE OF THINGS

"LaBute is the first dramatist since David Mamet and Sam Shepard—since Edward Albee, actually—to mix sympathy and savagery, pathos and power."   —Donald Lyons, *New York Post*

"LaBute . . . continues to probe the fascinating dark side of individualism . . . [His] great gift is to live in and to chronicle that murky area of not-knowing, which mankind spends much of its waking life denying."   —John Lahr, *The New Yorker*

"*Shape* . . . is LaBute's thesis on extreme feminine wiles, as well as a disquisition on how far an artist . . . can go in the name of art . . . Like a chiropractor of the soul, LaBute is looking for re-alignment, listening for a crack."   —John Istel, *Elle*

THE DISTANCE FROM HERE

"LaBute does not trivialize darkness but treats it with proper awe . . . In his most ambitious and best play to date, [he] gets inside the emptiness of American culture, the masquerade of pleasure and the evil of neglect. *The Distance from Here* . . . is a new title to be added to the short list of important contemporary plays."   —John Lahr, *The New Yorker*

"A bold dramatic concept . . . [*The Distance from Here*'s] trailer trash characters are keenly observed through the fug of ciga-rette smoke and beer fumes that envelops their native habitat."
                —Marilyn Stasio, *Variety*

BASH: LATTERDAY PLAYS

"Transfixing . . . In rendering these narratives, Mr. LaBute shows not only a merciless ear for contemporary speech but also a poet's sense of recurring, slyly graduated imagery . . . Unmistak-ably American . . . *Bash* is informed with an earnest, probing moralism as fierce as that of Nathaniel Hawthorne."
                —Ben Brantley, *The New York Times*

"Excellent . . . The fearsome power [of] this drama [is] meticu-lously crafted, so that the horror of the crimes creeps up and then slams in."   —Richard Christiansen, *Chicago Tribune*

"Captivating . . . LaBute's subtle poetry . . . arouse[s] a deeply disturbing emotional response."   —Steven Oxman, *Variety*

NEIL LABUTE

Fat Pig

NEIL LABUTE is a critically acclaimed playwright, filmmaker, and fiction writer. His controversial works include the plays *bash: latterday plays*, *The Distance from Here*, *The Mercy Seat* (Faber, 2003), *Autobahn* (Faber, 2005), and *This Is How It Goes* (Faber, 2005); the films *In the Company of Men* (Faber, 1997), *Your Friends and Neighbors* (Faber, 1998), *Nurse Betty*, and *Possession*; the play and film adaptation of *The Shape of Things* (Faber, 2001); and the short-story collection *Seconds of Pleasure*.

OTHER WORKS BY NEIL LABUTE AVAILABLE FROM FABER

In the Company of Men

Your Friends and Neighbors

The Shape of Things

The Mercy Seat

Autobahn

This Is How It Goes

Fat Pig

Fat Pig

a play by Neil LaBute

FARRAR, STRAUS AND GIROUX

NEW YORK

Farrar, Straus and Giroux
18 West 18th Street, New York 10011

Library of Congress Control Number: 2004110157
ISBN: 978-0-571-21150-0

Designed by Gretchen Achilles

Our books may be purchased in bulk for promotional, educational, or
business use. Please contact your local bookseller or the Macmillan Corporate
and Premium Sales Department at 1-800-221-7945, extension 5442,
or by e-mail at MacmillanSpecialMarkets@macmillan.com.

www.fsgbooks.com
www.twitter.com/fsgbooks • www.facebook.com/fsgbooks

21 23 25 26 24 22 20

For David Mamet

Take all away from me, but leave me Ecstasy . . .

—EMILY DICKINSON

You're the One for me, fatty . . .

—MORRISSEY

Preface: The Weight of the World

It was easy enough to lose, I suppose. The weight, I mean. One day I simply decided it was time, and I went about the process with a tenacity and diligence unheard-of for me. Unlike Adam, the protagonist of my 2001 play *The Shape of Things*, who is led down the path toward self-improvement by his interest in a young woman, my journey was a singular pursuit that was spurred on by more mundane reasons. I didn't feel so hot. I looked like shit. I was tired of wearing the same pants. So I did something about it.

I set up a rather specific regimen for myself and got down to the task at hand by using this simple mantra: "Stop eating so damn much, you fat bastard." Now, that sounds pretty basic and not very scientific, but I swear it was at the heart of my program. Alter a few basic ingredients and the recipe was bound to change, right? If I stopped gobbling down so much food (and a certain kind at that), started exercising a little, and gave it some time, my body would have no choice but to follow along. I didn't read the Atkins book or consult anyone in the medical profession; I simply decided to go for it. And I did just that—I dropped sixty pounds over the course of the next eight months and could see a marked difference in my attitude, body, and overall demeanor. I was happy, healthy, and in good spirits. Or so I thought.

Like the main character in that play, I also discovered the

preening fool who was living just beneath the surface of my usual self. Suddenly, the mirror became my friend. How I loved to rush home from a walk or jump up in the morning and study myself, checking to see if I looked a bit thinner. The day-to-day changes were imperceptible, of course, but that didn't stop me from slowing at every reflection or feeling my waistline or secretly patting my own ass to see if it was growing tighter or not. Who was this person? Not me, or at least it never had been me before this. But now here I was, stopping in at Banana Republic to try on new sweaters and secretly hoping I could drop one more waist size, just for fun. Taking my second long walk of the day simply because I had a free hour. This low-carb, heavy workout cycle was becoming as addictive to me as food had ever been, and I didn't see an end in sight. I also noticed that I was writing less and less.

The end, of course, came in the same way it does for so many people. Six months later I've gained back forty pounds, and I don't see that trend stopping anytime soon. Adam's first impulse when he discovers the deception of his girlfriend, Evelyn, is to eat. The stage directions ask for the character to shovel a few cookies into his mouth. "Look what I've been missing all this time," he seems to say. Like my fictional creation, I'm a stress eater. When things get bad or even slightly tricky, I reach for a bag of chips or a bucket of popcorn and hunker down. My mother taught me this self-medicating trick years ago, and I've stood by it for a long time now. When in doubt, eat some Pringles. A few personal and professional mishaps led me straight back to the pantry and right off the beaten path. Or any path, for that matter. I can't remember the last time I exercised. And I'm back wearing those same pants again, thank you very much for asking. Oh, yeah, and I've also written several new plays. One of them with the jaunty title of *Fat Pig*. Now, I'm not saying that creativity is entirely linked to personal unhappiness, but I remember reading with awe and respect the stories about Eugene O'Neill crying out behind closed doors and clawing at his own face as he composed *Long Day's Journey into Night*. Nothing of the sort happened here, of course, but you can definitely hear the crunch and crackle of snack food being consumed during some of my best work.

Which is what interests me so much about writing, I suppose. This notion of creation and how easy it is to make everything work out on paper. Unlike the character of Helen—the overweight, sensible, and perfectly lovely heroine of *Fat Pig* who disdains fiction for reality—I find things so much easier on the page than in real life. Want to visit the beach and not actually sweat or get sand in your hair? Start writing. Want to conjure up an unlikely but delightful romance without having to deal with the ramifications and fallout? Pick up your pen. It's an interesting anomaly: I love to make life unpredictable for a lot of my fictional characters as they face terrible mishaps, calamities, and upheavals, but more and more I find myself going to the computer to live out life rather than dealing with it. Writers, for better or worse, are gods of their own universe: "It is so because I say it's so." And while it might be a bit lonely In this particular heaven, I've got a terrific view. On paper, nobody complains as they climb a flight of stairs unless it's by my design. No one betrays a friend or lover unless I give the "all clear" sign. Life should be so easy.

As this play headed to New York for its premiere, it prompted a certain amount of introspection. I've often been asked who I see myself as when I write, which character is really me. In the past, I've been coy or clever or a bit of a smart-ass about it, falling back on that tired adage "There's a bit of me in all of them." In this case, though, I suppose it's true. But not just a bit. I see a lot of myself in *Fat Pig*; whatever the name of the piece, the story really deals with human weakness and the difficulty many people face when trying to stand up for, live up to, or come out for something they believe in. And that's pretty much me in a nutshell—well-meaning as can be, but surprisingly lame when push really comes to shove. Heroism, it would seem, is a tough gig.

As for the characters who populate *Fat Pig*, I love them all because they are so desperately human—they want to have convictions but, in the end, they'd rather be liked or get their needs met. They're not conventionally likeable, perhaps, but they're absolutely recognizable as people. Actually, I don't ever worry too much about the audience liking my characters or wanting to see them in a sequel or buying some merchandise related to the show. Leave that to the movies. All I care about is creating individuals who are interesting. Interesting and as complex as people are in life. I hope I've done that here.

NEIL LABUTE
SUMMER 2004

Fat Pig

Production History

Fat Pig had its world premiere on November 17, 2004, at the Manhattan Class Company (MCC) Theater in New York City. Director: Jo Bonney. Artistic Directors: Robert LuPone and Bernard Telsey. Associate Artistic Director: William Cantler. Executive Director: John G. Schultz. Set Design: Louisa Thompson; Costume Design: Mimi O'Donnell; Lighting Design: Matt Frey; Original Music and Sound Design: Robert Kaplowitz. Fight Director: Rick Sordelet. Production Stage Manager: Joel Rosen. Production Manager: B. D. White. Press Representative: Boneau/Bryan-Brown. Casting: Bernard Telsey Casting.

The cast was as follows:

HELEN	ASHLIE ATKINSON
TOM	JEREMY PIVEN
CARTER	ANDREW MCCARTHY
JEANNIE	KERI RUSSELL

Characters

HELEN

TOM

CARTER

JEANNIE

Setting

A big city near the ocean

"That First Meeting with Her"

A WOMAN *in a crowded restaurant, standing at one of those tall tables. A bunch of food in front of her, and she is quietly eating it. By the way, she's a plus size. Very.*

After a moment, a MAN *enters, juggling a lunch tray. He looks around, then moves toward her.*

MAN . . . pretty big.

WOMAN Excuse me?

MAN I'm sorry, I was just sort of, you know, speaking out loud. Pretty big in here. That's what I was saying . . .

WOMAN Oh. Right.

MAN Lots of room for, you know, *people.*

WOMAN Yes. It's popular.

The MAN *looks around, trying to see if there's a spot for him yet.*

WOMAN You can eat here if you want.

MAN No, I don't need to, umm . . .

WOMAN What?

MAN I dunno, I hadn't really thought the rest of that one through! Ahh, "intrude," I guess.

WOMAN You're not. I'll make some room for you.

MAN You sure?

WOMAN Of course.

MAN Thanks.

She stares at him a minute, then slides some of her food to one side, allowing him a space if he wants it.

WOMAN I thought you meant me. Before.

MAN I'm sorry?

WOMAN When you said that, "pretty big," I thought you were saying that to me. *About* me.

MAN Oh, no, God, no! I wouldn't . . . You did?

WOMAN For a second.

MAN No, that'd be . . . you know. Rude.

WOMAN Still . . .

MAN I mean, why would I do that? A thing like that? I'm not . . .

WOMAN You'd be surprised. People say all kinds of things here.

MAN In this place?

WOMAN No, not just *here*, this restaurant or anything, I mean in the city.

MAN So . . . you mean, people actually . . . what? Say things to your face?

WOMAN Of course. All the time.

MAN About what?

She looks over at him without saying anything. Silence.

WOMAN . . . My *hair color*. (*Beat.*) What do you think?

MAN Oh, I see. (*Smiles.*) Sure . . .

WOMAN It's not a huge deal—I was just mentioning it.

MAN Yeah, but . . .

Neil LaBute

WOMAN You get used to it. I guess they think that—I don't know, after a certain size or whatever . . .

MAN Geez, that's hard to . . .

WOMAN I shouldn't have all this stuff for lunch, anyway, but I can't help it. I'm hungry.

MAN Sure . . . hey, it's lunchtime, right?

WOMAN Yeah.

MAN I mean, look at me . . . look how much *chicken* they put on my salad!

WOMAN That's not exactly comforting . . .

MAN I just meant . . . whatever. Sorry.

WOMAN I had three pieces of pizza, and the garlic bread, and a salad. Plus dessert . . .

MAN Hey, you know . . . It's your . . .

WOMAN How does that sentence end?

MAN Badly, I'm sure! Hell, it's your body, you do what you want. That's what I think . . .

WOMAN Really?

MAN Of course. I mean . . .

WOMAN So, do you really like *sprouts* or does that only hold true for me? Your little theory there . . .

MAN No, I'm just . . . I had a really big breakfast, so I'm . . .

WOMAN That's a lie.

MAN Ahh, yeah. Yes, it was. You saw through that one . . . Damn, you seem pretty good at this!

WOMAN What, the truth?

MAN Yeah, that.

WOMAN I'm not bad, actually . . . not too bad at all.

A moment between them; then they both get down to some serious eating.

WOMAN Yes, I'm over at the library. I was at an interview, actually, for a different branch . . . that's why I have the, you know, "Miss Kitty" hair today, All *dolled* up.

The MAN *nods and points at a plastic bag on the table.*

MAN Ahh, cool . . . I get it. *Gunsmoke.* You look nice. (*Grins.*) Yeah, I saw the library bag earlier. Thought maybe you just stopped by there and checked those out, or . . .

WOMAN Nope. "I'm not just the president, I'm also a client . . . " (*Beat.*) That one wig commercial? The Hair Club for Men or something . . .

MAN Oh, right . . . right! (*Laughs.*) That's funny. Yeah. Who do they think is really gonna fall for that stuff?

WOMAN I dunno! It always looks so cheesy when guys do that . . . people should just go with it, you know? I mean, whatever they look like. It's . . .

MAN Yeah. I agree. (*Points.*) That's a *lot* of videos there.

WOMAN It was a long weekend . . .

MAN Right. (*Smiles.*) So, lemme guess . . . *When Harry Met Sally, Sleepless in Seattle*, probably, ummm . . .

WOMAN Wrong. Take a look.

She smiles at him as he reaches over and glances in the bag. Pulls a few out. Library emblem on each case.

MAN *The Guns of Navarone, Where Eagles Dare . . . Ice Station Zebra?*

WOMAN I threw myself a little Alistair MacLean festival.

MAN Huh. Don't get me wrong, because I love that stuff, but . . . that's not very "girlie" of you.

WOMAN You're probably just dating the wrong *kinds* of girls.

They share a smile and a chuckle. The MAN *reappraises her.*

MAN No doubt about that—I can't even call 'em "girls" without getting hit by a *lawsuit*, so . . . (*Grins.*) You're a librarian?

WOMAN Yeah. Well, we don't really use that term anymore, but, ahh . . .

MAN Sure, of course! It's probably, like, "printed-word specialist" or something now, I suppose . . .

WOMAN Exactly. (*Beat.*) They're always coming up with new names for stuff, something to make that person feel better . . . a "refuse technician" or what have you.

MAN That's so true . . .

WOMAN Right? Problem is, you still find yourself picking *shit* up off the street, no matter what they call you! I mean . . . you know . . .

He laughs at this, and she joins in. The MAN *studies her.*

MAN You have a terrific laugh.

WOMAN Thanks.

MAN You're welcome. A *potty mouth*, but a really cute laugh . . .

WOMAN That's sweet, thank you! (*Laughs.*) Now that I'm so self-conscious that I'll never do it again . . .

MAN Exactly!

They smile at each other and then don't know what to say next. They decide to take bites of their meals instead.

WOMAN How's that *spinach* coming along?

MAN Mmmmmmmm . . . so darn good.

WOMAN I bet.

MAN Yeah. Yummy.

WOMAN The pizza's terrific here. I come by all the time for it . . .

MAN I'll bet. (*Looks over at her.*) I just mean . . . you know. If it's so good, I would understand. That. (*Beat.*) Please-help-me.

WOMAN I get what you meant.

MAN Great.

WOMAN You shouldn't be so nervous . . . I mean, if we're gonna start dating.

MAN *What?*

WOMAN I'm kidding.

MAN Oh, right. Got it. Little slow!

They laugh together. He looks around, self-consciously.

WOMAN I'm sorry. You should've seen your face . . .

MAN What? No . . .

WOMAN I thought you were gonna choke on your *avocado* there . . .

MAN That's not true, come on . . .

WOMAN Pretty close.

MAN No, that's not . . . why would you say that? You just caught me off guard is all. Seriously.

WOMAN Anyway, I was just playing. Big people are *jolly*, remember?

MAN Ummm-hmmm . . .

WOMAN It's one of our best qualities.

MAN Well, at least you've got one.

WOMAN And you don't?

MAN Ahhh . . . open for debate.

WOMAN Really?

MAN I mean . . . you know, if I really had to come up with one, for, say, the big guy upstairs or whatever, I'd probably do something like "does not run with scissors" or one of those. "Plays well with others."

WOMAN Really? Handsome guy like you and that's all you're good for . . . to look at?

MAN Pretty much.

WOMAN Good to know. (*Opens a pudding.*) You want one?

MAN Nah, I shouldn't . . .

WOMAN Why?

MAN Excellent question. Okay.

He takes a tub of rice pudding from her and digs in.

WOMAN Good?

MAN Mmmmmmm . . . wonderful. Haven't done that in ages.

WOMAN What?

MAN Enjoyed myself. Like that. Put something in my mouth without reading the back label like some *Bible scholar* . . .

He gives an example—holding the pudding up to the light as if it was an antiquity and squinting at it. Examining it from all angles. This makes her laugh again. A lot.

MAN All right, okay, we're gonna have to ask you to leave . . . You're actually enjoying yourself during the workweek.

WOMAN Right! Sorry . . .

MAN No, I told you, I love your laugh. It's okay.

WOMAN Thanks. Again.

MAN You're welcome . . .

WOMAN So . . . no other good qualities, huh?

MAN Ahhhhh, I suppose. Faithful friend and co-worker, dependable, takes directions well.

WOMAN What about good lover? Not on the list?

The MAN *stares at her, glances around. She keeps looking right at him.*

MAN That's very direct . . .

WOMAN Librarians are funny people.

MAN I *guess* . . . I shouldn't've let my card lapse!

WOMAN No, look what you've been missing.

MAN Yeah.

WOMAN So?

MAN Ummm . . . I'm okay. I mean, no reports of absolute dissatisfaction, but I don't think I'm, like, Valentino or anything.

WOMAN You mean the movie guy? *The Sheik* or whatever?

MAN Yep. Wasn't he like this big Latin lover or something?

WOMAN I guess that was the story . . . He died really unhappy, though. I've read his biography.

MAN One of the perks of the job . . .

WOMAN Right! I've read just about every biography in the place, actually. Real people interest me. I don't really have much time for fiction. "Fiction is for the weak and faint of heart." Somebody said that. A Frenchman, I think.

MAN Cool . . .

WOMAN Anyway, you don't have to answer the question. It was rude.

MAN No, I . . . I mean, I sort of did.

WOMAN And you're what? Just okay?

MAN Something like that . . . I do fine. Wow. I've never . . . been asked that before. In *that* way.

WOMAN No?

MAN Not at lunch, anyhow! (*Beat.*) It's kind of invigorating, actually. You seem like a really . . . I don't know. An interesting person, I guess.

They laugh together again. Really enjoying themselves.

WOMAN You should swing by the library sometime. See what you've been missing . . .

MAN Yeah. (*Beat.*) Listen, I'm . . . I need to get back to the office. Downtown. So I should finish up my, ahh . . .

WOMAN All right. Sorry if I was . . .

MAN No, no, it was . . . but could we . . . I dunno what I'm asking here. Should we see each other again?

WOMAN Why?

MAN I dunno . . . I mean, I'm just, it'd be good, I think. You seem really nice and I'm . . . what can I say, I'm just asking . . . sort of outta the blue. So, could we? (*Beat.*) I'm not trying to pick you up or anything, I just . . .

WOMAN Too bad. (*Smiles.*) Yes. We should.

MAN For lunch? Or, ummm, dinner . . . ?

WOMAN I don't *only* eat. I can be coaxed into doing other stuff, too . . .

MAN Of course! I didn't mean . . .

WOMAN I know. It's a joke.

MAN Right, sure . . . I'm really striking out on the humor part here.

WOMAN You're doing fine . . . (*Beat.*) So when?

MAN Anytime.

WOMAN How about Friday? I'm good for Fridays, my day off.

MAN Ummm, yeah. Evening.

WOMAN Great.

She reaches over and takes a pen out of his shirt pocket and writes her number down on the side of a napkin.

WOMAN Now when you wipe your mouth you'll think of me . . .

MAN Good plan. (*Beat.*) So, okay, library lady, I'll call you . . .

WOMAN Helen. My name's Helen.

MAN As in "of Troy"? (*Groans.*) That was so lame, sorry . . .

HELEN Right, the thousand ships and all. But that was just so they could carry me back . . .

He stands there, thinking about this. Doesn't get it.

HELEN . . . because it would take that many to lift me . . . Don't worry about it.

MAN Oh, I see. (*Laughs.*) I got it!

HELEN Yeah. Just trying to be cute.

MAN No, yes, I get it now . . . but you shouldn't do that, though. Make fun of yourself so much.

HELEN Why not?

MAN Ummmmmm . . . I'm sure there's a very good reason. I'll get back to you.

HELEN You do that. You've got the number there . . .

MAN Right. I'll call you. And I'm Tom, by the way.

HELEN I'll see you. Tom.

Neil LaBute

She wanders off with her tray and her bag. TOM *stands alone. After a moment, she returns. Walks right up to him and gets close.*

HELEN So, look, I figure there's every reason why I'll never hear from you again, and that's why I came back here, just to say that I don't do this, come after guys or anything, not like some regular habit or whatever, so I thought you should know that. I think you're really cute and nice and that sort of thing . . . you might have a girlfriend already or not be attracted to me, I would just totally understand that, I would, but I really do hope you call me. Just even to talk on the phone would be fine, because I'd like that, if we were only these phone buddies . . . I think I would. Just don't be afraid, Tom, I guess that's why I came back here, to say that. Please do not let yourself be afraid of me or of taking some kind of blind chance, or what people think . . . because this could be so great.

She smiles at him and does what she promised: wanders out of the joint. He watches her go, waves when she nears the door.

TOM *goes back to eating the pudding and then looks up, off in the direction that she left. He slowly folds the napkin up and pockets it.*

"The Work Friends Figure It Out"

TOM *at his place of work. Busy doing something. Another guy enters, carrying some files and a cup of coffee. He throws himself down in a chair. His name is* CARTER.

CARTER . . . So you're not gonna tell me, right? Anything else, I mean.

TOM No, I'll . . . you know . . .

CARTER Uh-uh, no, you won't. I know you.

TOM That's not true, I always tell you crap! All kinds of crap about me.

CARTER Yeah, but not the good stuff that I wanna hear. The dirt.

TOM I don't have *dirt* . . .

CARTER Everybody's got dirt, my friend! We're dirty, us folks. Very dirty.

TOM Who's "us folks"?

CARTER People. You and me–type people.

TOM It's not . . . this is not some nasty thing that I'm trying to keep from you. Seriously.

CARTER Okay then, so?

TOM This is just . . . it's new, that's all. I don't know what it is yet, so . . .

CARTER So, like I said, you're not gonna tell me shit.

TOM Kinda. Yeah.

CARTER Fine. I don't care.

TOM Bull . . . you're dying to hear.

CARTER Yes, but I'll wait. I'll hire some private eye or whatnot, find the scoop that way. Whatever it takes . . .

TOM Come on . . . I just wanna see what it is first. If it's worth talking to anyone about or not. (*Beat.*) What I will say is, I'm very happy right now . . .

CARTER Okay, now you're frightening me . . .

TOM What?

CARTER I don't like it when you get all serious! Then it's like *girlfriend city*, and that's scary.

TOM It's not scary . . .

CARTER This is when we lose you for weeks at a time. Tom gets a lady friend, and he drops off the map, I know how this one works . . .

TOM I'm not at all like that!

CARTER Yes, you are . . .

TOM No, uh-uh. If anybody is, you are.

CARTER Yeah, but that's for good reason. I'm actually having sex with them.

TOM Very funny.

CARTER Seriously.

TOM Shut the hell up! I have sex . . .

CARTER Uh-uh, "oral" doesn't count. And especially not for somebody who thinks it means *talking* a person to death . . .

TOM Hooooo . . . funny! (*Beat.*) Are you in here for an actual reason?

CARTER Pretty much. I don't remember what it is, but I'm sure I had one when I started down the hall . . .

TOM Perfect.

CARTER Oh, yeah, now I recall. Because I was bored in my office . . . (*Beat.*) Plus, you have nicer windows.

TOM Feel free to open one and jump . . .

CARTER You are so clever!

TOM Seriously, though, I've got work.

CARTER I've got work, too. We've all got work, Tom, that's why they call it that. "Work." Because that's what we do here.

TOM I agree. And I want to get back to mine . . .

CARTER Fine. (*Picks up a ball.*) Dollar a point?

TOM *nods, and the two men break into a lazy game of Nerf "pig." The hoop hangs on the back of* TOM*'s door.*

A female CO-WORKER *walks in, carrying a stack of reports—ruins the game. She stops at* TOM*'s desk and drops a few files. Smiles.* CARTER *eyes her, then speaks.*

CARTER Guess what?

CO-WORKER What?

CARTER I said *guess.*

CO-WORKER Ummm . . . you're an asshole?

TOM *giggles out loud at this one.* CARTER *blushes, then regroups. The girl smiles over at* TOM.

TOM Aaah, you cheated! Somebody gave you the answers . . .

CO-WORKER Exactly. (*Grins.*) Morning, Tom . . .

CARTER You guys are hilarious.

CO-WORKER What is it? I need to get back.

CARTER Okay, then don't worry about it.

CO-WORKER Just tell me. *What?*

CARTER Tom's got a gal.

TOM Would you shut up!

CARTER Word on the street . . .

TOM Carter, seriously . . .

CO-WORKER Really? (*to* TOM) That's not true, right?

TOM No . . . he's just being a dick.

CARTER Am not! I mean, yes, I am a dick sometimes, but not at the moment.

CO-WORKER Tom . . . ?

CARTER He does.

⌈**TOM** I do *not*. (*to her*) Jeannie, he's just trying to . . .

⌊**CARTER** It's what I heard . . .

TOM Carter, knock it off.

JEANNIE *stands there for a bit longer, looking back and forth between the men. Finally, she saunters out.*

TOM You prick.

CARTER *What?*

TOM That's not funny.

CARTER It was pretty damn funny from over here . . .

TOM I'm serious.

CARTER Me, too. Try sitting on the couch and see if it's any funnier. (*He moves over.*) Plenty of room.

TOM You know we've been dating . . . sort of.

CARTER Of course. I-know-all.

TOM I mean it. I said how she gets.

CARTER Yes, I *know* . . . (*Beat.*) Why do you think I said something? I'm not gonna tell the *snack-shop guy* out front . . . I mean, why the fuck would he care?

TOM You are a piece of work, you know that?

CARTER I try. (*Beat.*) Anyway, that's what you can expect, by the way. Mean-spirited shit like that until you tell me who she is.

TOM I'm not gonna say a damn thing now . . .

CARTER Your choice. But I'll find out, I promise . . .

TOM Yeah, yeah . . .

CARTER And then up goes her Polaroid in the break room.

TOM Fucker.

CARTER Maybe. After you're through with her, of course . . .

TOM Shut up and go back to your *lair*, Satan.

CARTER Fair enough. (*Beat.*) Hey, seriously though . . . does Jeannie look kind of soft to you?

TOM What?

CARTER A minute ago . . . doesn't she look a bit sloppy or something? In her ass, I'm saying. Flabby.

TOM No . . .

CARTER Come on, I'm just talking. It's not a judgment on you.

TOM I know, but . . . I'm not obsessed by bodies the way you are. I'm not.

CARTER I don't know what it is, but I was noticing yesterday. She came into my office with her suit jacket off and had on one of those, you know, flimsy sort of blouses with the no-sleeves look. I seriously think her arms have gotten chunkier or whatever. The past few months.

TOM Dude, you need some help . . .

CARTER What? It's an observation, that's all . . . her arms. The ass. I can't help it if I observe things.

TOM No, but you can keep it to yourself! And your therapist, who I hope you're still seeing . . .

CARTER Nah, that shit was too expensive. Plus, she was a total bitch.

TOM Nice.

CARTER It's not, like, some derogatory thing I'm saying about her—not the therapist cunt, but Jeannie—it's just an idle thought. She seems to be packing it on some. That's the problem with winter: chicks don't get out much and they bloat up . . .

TOM Okay, I really can't deal with you right now, so . . . go.

CARTER Whatever. We on for basketball Friday? Chad can't make it any other time . . .

TOM Ahh, yeah. But after nine, okay? I've got a dinner thing. (*off of* CARTER *'s look*) For *work*, dumbshit.

CARTER Sure.

TOM It is! I've got those folks from the, ahhh . . . you know . . .

CARTER No, what?

TOM The Chicago group is coming into town. (*Beat.*) They *are* . . .

CARTER Cool. I'll e-mail the other guys and meet you at the Y. See ya.

CARTER *finally gets up and saunters over to* TOM—*a quick high five and* CARTER *exits.* TOM *returns to his work as* CARTER *looks back inside the room.*

CARTER I'm swinging past the restaurant to check, so you better be telling the truth . . .

TOM Asshole.

CARTER That's me. But when I get my Ph.D. it'll be Doctor Asshole, so, hey. Something to look forward to . . .

He is gone. TOM *shakes his head and gets back to the files that* JEANNIE *has left. A minute later, he looks up to see her standing in his doorway.*

JEANNIE Hey. (*Smiles.*) Got a minute?

TOM Oh, hi. There.

JEANNIE I forgot some . . . here. (*Holds up an extra file.*) Forgot this one.

TOM Ah. Thanks. Ummmm . . .

TOM *gets up and crosses to her, reaching for the folder. She holds it a moment, and they both tug on it.*

JEANNIE So . . . is it true, what he said?

TOM Who, Carter?

JEANNIE Yeah.

TOM Ummm . . .

JEANNIE Oh. (*Beat.*) So where does that put us, then? I mean, I thought—

TOM No, I'm not saying it's . . . he's an idiot, so, you know, you have to make some allowances.

JEANNIE Right. (*Grins.*) That's true . . .

TOM But . . . I don't know what I'm doing. You know that. I'm—

JEANNIE Yes, I do. All while we were going out I could tell that, but I still liked you. Gave you a million or so chances, but . . . hey. Whatever.

TOM I know that, Jeannie, I know, I'm just . . . it's complicated.

JEANNIE I'm not saying that I'm some, you know, *glamour queen*, but guys do like me. They do.

TOM I know, come on . . . *please*. I like you. Don't say it like that.

JEANNIE Yeah, well . . . I wish you'd fire up a signal flare every now and then. (*Smiles.*) Could use it over here.

TOM Sorry. I do, though.

JEANNIE Doesn't seem like it. I mean, I've tried sweet and forceful and, you know, *nonchalant* . . . everything. I don't get it. What do you want me to do here?

TOM *Nothing.* I'm—

JEANNIE *What?* (*Beat.*) So, just tell me. Is he lying or not?

TOM Carter is . . . I mean, by nature he's a liar. You know that. He likes to provoke people. Get 'em riled up.

JEANNIE Which says nothing.

TOM Jeannie, come on . . .

JEANNIE So you are.

TOM I'm not . . . no. I'm not "seeing" any other person, all right? Promise.

JEANNIE Look, I'm just asking, so don't make it seem like I'm pulling on your eyeteeth or something. If you don't wanna tell me, then okay.

TOM I'm saying it, to you, right now.

JEANNIE Yeah, but . . .

TOM Carter's an ass. He's . . .

JEANNIE So why do you hang out with him then? Huh? All those guys down in Development. (*Beat.*) Why?

TOM Because . . . I'm needy and shallow. (*Smiles.*) Hell, I dunno! Because we all . . . started out here together, and it's, you know, it's easier to go along sometimes, to just hang out and not make, like, some big tsunami or that kind of thing. I know it's dumb, but . . . he's *funny.* He doesn't bug me that much.

JEANNIE Obviously.

TOM Jeannie, come on, don't be . . . he's just playing around.

JEANNIE So, nobody then?

TOM I didn't . . . I'm not saying . . . What?

JEANNIE Don't do your circles thing, okay? Do not do that—

TOM What're you even—?

JEANNIE Talking around shit, that's what I'm saying. I hate that! Are-you-dating-someone?

TOM No. Kind of. Hell, I dunno! I'm . . . It's not some big thing.

JEANNIE I see.

TOM Look, we said that we could . . . I'm not doing anything, like, *wrong*.

JEANNIE But you're pretty defensive about it.

TOM Yeah, because . . . because you get all . . . you know how you are.

JEANNIE I'm not *anything*. Except confused. By a guy who tells me that he's interested in me. "Very," in fact, was the word he used. "I am very interested in you." And we date, and then we stop, and then he sends me stuff, like flowers and letters, and keeps calling and wants to do it again, to try one more time, he tells me . . . but then we do not go out. We see each other at work, but he keeps putting off the next date because of . . . God, I couldn't begin to list all of the excuses because it's Monday afternoon, and I would probably be here, like, through the *weekend*. But now I hear he's met someone, a someone who he has managed—even with his many work obligations and boys' nights out and all his other related *juvenile* shit—he has somehow squeezed yet another person onto his social calendar.

JEANNIE *edges a bit closer to* TOM *now.* TOM *steps back.*

TOM See? This is what I was talking about.

JEANNIE No, this is what *I'm* talking about right now! The bullshit you do to me and expect me to keep crawling back in here and taking it.

TOM I don't . . . want you to . . .

JEANNIE Oh, so now you don't want me here? Is that it? Go ahead, then, say it. Go on. Say-it.

TOM No, Jeannie, Jesus, can we just . . . I'd like to talk about this, but not in public. All right? I mean, can we . . . maybe . . .

JEANNIE You can "maybe" kiss my ass, Tom, and that's a *definite* maybe. We can *pencil* that one in my planner right now, okay?

JEANNIE *turns abruptly and walks out. Before* TOM *can even react, she is back. Standing in the doorway.*

TOM Jeannie, please. Let's . . .

JEANNIE I can't *wait* to meet her. Really, I can't. (*Holds out file.*) I forgot to give you this.

TOM *moves apprehensively toward the door.* JEANNIE *drops the file onto the floor and stalks off.*

"A Surprising Night Out Together"

TOM *and* HELEN *sitting at a table in a cozy restaurant. A meal spread out before them.* TOM *is chowing down on exotic cuisine;* HELEN *is a bit more hesitant.*

TOM . . . Go on, jump in there. (*Prompts her.*) Be brave.

HELEN You're absolutely sure it's dead, right? Because if it's just holding its breath, then I'm . . .

TOM Yeah! (*Laughs.*) Definitely . . .

HELEN Okay. (*Looks again.*) Positive?

TOM Well, I wasn't back there watching 'em fix it but, yeah, in theory.

HELEN I mean, I'm pretty *adventurous*, but, you know . . .

TOM No, I'm the same way. It's . . . I'm not big on swallowing anything I saw on Discovery Channel either, believe me . . . (*Smiles.*) It's good. Promise.

HELEN *smiles and nods, gobbles something down with her eyes closed. Happy with the results.* TOM *smiles as he eats something, too. Lets a moment of silence hang.*

TOM Can I ask you something?

HELEN Sure, what?

TOM I meant to ask you this the other night . . . I mean, when we went to that martini bar . . . (*Beat.*) You love war movies?

HELEN *smiles over at him and nods. Says nothing else.*

TOM Okay, first obvious question. *Why?*

HELEN Just because.

TOM Uh-uh, no, not fair! That's not an answer . . .

HELEN Yes, it is.

TOM But not a good one. One that tells me anything about
  you . . .

HELEN Ohhh, I see. You're gonna dig deep now, is that it?

TOM Something like that . . .

HELEN All right, fine. (*Beat.*) I like war movies because . . . all
  the pretty explosions.

This makes TOM *laugh, and he reaches out for* HELEN*'s hand. He
grabs it and squeezes, holding on to it. She notices.*

TOM Come on! Seriously . . .

HELEN Okay, okay . . . I'm . . . (*Beat.*) You have my hand there,
  you know.

TOM Yeah, I . . . is that not . . . ?

HELEN It's fine. Just wanted to ask and see if it was an
  accident or not.

TOM Umm . . . no. It wasn't, no. But . . . now you're making me
  self-conscious.

TOM *looks around the restaurant.* HELEN *notices this, too.*

TOM Silly. I want to, hold it, I mean, if that's okay.

HELEN Of course.

TOM Good.

They sit and stare at each other for a moment. Silence.

HELEN I would like to have a bit more of my tuna later . . . but I
can wait.

TOM Sorry! Shit . . .

HELEN I'm kidding you.

TOM *looks at her, then pulls away, embarrassed. He points at
her food.*

TOM No, you should . . . that's fine. We can do that after, or
walking back to the car or something. We should eat. Yes.

HELEN Tom . . . I really was joking.

TOM I know, but . . . (*He eats.*) I'm ready for some of mine, too.

HELEN All right. (*Looking into bowl.*) Is it smiling at me, or am
I . . . ?

TOM No . . . (*Glances in.*) That's an *eye*. He's winking at you,
be nice . . .

They both take a bite or two, laughing across the table.

TOM So, seriously . . . what's the deal on the war flicks? You
know way too many of those things to've just been reading
the *TV Guide* or that kind of thing . . .

HELEN Please, I'm a professional.

TOM Oh, yeah? Prove it.

HELEN Let's see if you can keep up. *Von Ryan's . . . Von
Ryan's . . .*

TOM *Train . . .* No, wait . . . *Express!*

HELEN *Lonely Are the . . .*

TOM *Brave.*

HELEN *Heaven Knows, Mr. . . .*

TOM Magoo!

HELEN No, *Allison.*

TOM Jesus . . . and most of those are obscure, too.

HELEN I know. (*Beat.*) I used to work in audiovisual.

TOM You're very . . . except that one.

HELEN Which?

TOM *Lonely Are the Brave.*

HELEN It's a . . . what?

TOM A western. Sort of, one of those modern kind. With Kirk
Douglas.

HELEN Oh, right, no, I mean . . . is it?

TOM Yeah. You know, with him on the horse, and he's being
chased by, like, guys in helicopters and stuff? It's that one.
It's really good, but, yeah. Western.

HELEN Huh. (*Considers.*) Oh, right, right, yes, I've seen it, but
I'm getting the name confused. I mean *None but the Brave.*
The Frank Sinatra one. On the atoll in the Pacific.

TOM You're . . . *nobody's* seen that one! All right, this is now,
like, an officially *quirky* side of you. (*Grins.*) "Atoll"?

HELEN Hey, I'm a librarian . . .

TOM Uh-uh. "Printed-word specialist."

HELEN Right! (*Laughs.*) Anyway, I grew up with 'em. That's all. I
have three brothers, plus my dad. They were on all the time,
and so I watched a lot of them, or parts of 'em, anyway. All
growing up.

TOM Yeah, me, too. I mean, that same scenario. What is it
about fathers and those movies? (*Beat.*) He also directed
that one, too.

HELEN Your father?

TOM No . . . Sinatra! You're funny.

HELEN Thanks.

TOM I mean, *jolly*. (*Beat*.) Kidding.

They both laugh again. Really enjoying each other now.

TOM But, seriously, I wonder. Why?

HELEN Well . . . most of them either fought in wars or wanted
to, or had some relative who did or whatever. Or they just
like watching other guys get shot, that could be it, too.

TOM Probably right! That sounds more accurate . . .

HELEN I'm not joking. I think guys today feel left out, like,
guilty about not having to kill things, provide food. All that
"early man" stuff. (*Beat*.) But for me . . . I just enjoyed being
around my family. Sitting on the couch, big bowl of popcorn.
It felt good.

TOM Right . . .

HELEN *And* it saved me the embarrassment of sitting around
waiting for boys to call me up.

TOM What do you mean?

HELEN Ummm, you probably couldn't guess, but I didn't date a
lot when I was in school.

TOM Oh.

HELEN (*whispers*) I used to be a touch *heavy*.

HELEN chuckles. TOM joins in halfheartedly, then stops.

TOM Huh. (*Beat*.) And is that . . . is it all right to talk about . . .
I dunno, your weight and everything, or should I . . . ?

HELEN No, go ahead. It's not a shame thing for me. Not
anymore.

TOM "Anymore"?

HELEN Well . . . it's all shame when you're younger, isn't it? You hate how you look or sound or, you know, all that stuff that we go through. As kids. But I'm pretty all right with who I am now. The trick is getting other people to be okay with it!

TOM Right. And, so . . . have you always been, like . . . you know?

HELEN No. What?

TOM Ummm, big . . . boned, or whatever.

HELEN *laughs out loud at this one. Another beauty, which makes* TOM *giggle along. She takes his hand this time.*

HELEN That was kind of precious. One of my favorites, actually.

TOM What?

HELEN "Big-boned." My mom used to throw that one around, too.

TOM Well . . . I'm just trying to be . . .

HELEN Don't. Not for me. I just want you to be truthful, all right? Seriously.

TOM Okay.

HELEN However things end up here—and I have high hopes, but— (*Smiles.*) I want you to be honest with me.

TOM I can do that. Promise.

HELEN Good. Great. Fair enough.

TOM So, then, ummm . . . I don't know what to say here exactly, but . . . (*Beat.*) . . . Helen, I like your body . . . what I *imagine* your body to be. It's . . .

HELEN Tom, It's *okay* . . . I'm not worried about it. I mean, you would not be here next to me, if you didn't want to be. Right?

TOM Sure. Yes.

HELEN So, then . . . I'm good. Secure about it. Truthfully. I know that you're here because you like me. A little bit, anyway.

TOM That's true. I do, yes. Like you.

HELEN Then good . . . (*Smiles.*) So, why don't we finish up our seafood . . . (*Thinks.*) . . . *stuff.* What's this called again.

TOM Ahh . . . you got the, umm, Yellowfin Tartare, and I got their, I don't remember now. Spicy Kimchi, maybe? With crab . . .

HELEN Yeah, that was it.

HELEN *smiles and touches his hand again, then goes back to eating.* TOM *watches her as she takes a few more bites.*

TOM How's your meal? Okay?

HELEN Delicious, actually. Little bit of ginger and scallions, I like it . . .

TOM Good. (*Waits.*) You know, the yellow-fin is traditionally the "biggest-boned" of the tuna family . . .

HELEN Oh really? (*Giggles.*) Tell me more.

TOM Seriously—with a hearty, heavy flavor . . .

HELEN *and* TOM *laugh together, their heads coming in close contact. Suddenly,* HELEN *notices that* TOM *is now staring off, behind her. She swings around and spots* CARTER, *a drink in one hand.* TOM *awkwardly stands up.*

TOM Hey . . .

CARTER Well, hello there.

TOM Carter, this is . . . Helen, I'd like you to meet my . . . this is Carter, who works with us. I mean, me.

HELEN *smiles and holds a hand up.* CARTER *takes it and shakes it. Looks around.*

CARTER Where's the rest of 'em? Late?

An uncomfortable moment hangs in the air. HELEN *begins to stand.*

HELEN I'm going to use the little girls' room. Even though I hate the term.
TOM Right! (*Tries to laugh.*) Me, too.
CARTER Well . . . it's better than "shitter."
HELEN Very true. (*Beat.*) Nice to meet you, Carter.
CARTER Yeah, you, too.

She walks off, and CARTER *watches her go—all the way offstage. He then turns to* TOM *and gestures.*

CARTER I hope it's *twins.* (*Smiles.*) Bet you're glad you promised to play basketball tonight, huh?
TOM Uh-huh.
CARTER Who the hell is that?
TOM I just told you. Her name's Helen, and she's . . . you know . . .
CARTER . . . and how come the others aren't here?
TOM Because we're . . . I mean . . .

CARTER *reaches over and pokes at* TOM *'s shirt. Giggles.*

CARTER Jesus . . . nice shirt there, buddy. They're gonna think we manufacture *mirror balls* or something.

TOM Very funny! I'm not . . . I hate doing a suit all the time. The whole *tie* thing . . .

CARTER Huh. O-kay. (*Beat.*) They didn't just send her, did they? Not that she couldn't eat for *five* . . .

TOM Carter, don't say stuff like that. It's not nice.

CARTER I know that. I wasn't being nice. That was me being honest.

TOM Seriously, though . . .

CARTER Hey, she's not here, okay, so can you ease up on the Knights of the Round Table shit? She's off to the bathroom . . . (*Beat.*) With a basket of dinner rolls hidden under her skirt, if I'm not mistaken . . .

TOM Can you please . . . ? Jesus.

CARTER Okay, all right. God, you are really just not fun at all when you're out with a woman, you know that? Even some *beast* from work . . .

TOM She's not . . . just leave her alone.

CARTER Fine. (*Beat.*) You gonna be there by nine? Howard's gotta hit the road by eleven-thirty . . .

TOM Yes, you know that . . . yes. (*looking around*) Why are you here?

CARTER I told you I was coming by.

TOM Yeah, but how'd you know where . . . ?

CARTER Because you always come here! But Tom? This place is kinda out of the loop, I hate to tell you. By, like, ahh, *three* years.

TOM Yeah, well, I like it. (*Beat.*) So, can I just finish up and . . . do you mind?

CARTER No, whatever. Just checking on ya.

TOM Fine.

CARTER Thought I might catch you with . . . you know. *Her*.

TOM You really are an ass . . .

CARTER Pretty much. But, surprisingly, it doesn't give me a big head . . .

TOM Will you just please go?! Come on.

CARTER Fine, fine. See you at nine.

TOM Yeah. See you.

CARTER *takes another gulp from his drink, then stops. He starts off but leans in close to* TOM.

CARTER Dude . . . I so wish I would've caught you with her! Damn it. Anyway . . .

At that moment, HELEN *returns and stands next to* CARTER. *He pulls out her chair and seats her.*

HELEN Thank you . . .

CARTER Pleasure. (*to* HELEN) And don't let this cheapskate stiff you on the dessert! They've got a hell of a green tea ice cream here . . .

HELEN Good to know . . .

TOM See you later, Carter.

HELEN Good-bye. Nice to meet you.

CARTER You, too, ummm . . . what was it again?

HELEN Helen.

CARTER Right. (*over his shoulder*) And say hello to the Windy City for me!

CARTER is gone. TOM *watches him go and then turns back to* HELEN. *Tries to smile.*

HELEN What does that mean?

TOM He's . . . you know, he's a . . .

HELEN Why would he think I'm from there? Chicago?

TOM He doesn't. No. That was for me. *To* me. I'm . . . going there for work.

HELEN Really?

TOM For, like, yeah. Just a day or two next week. Business.

HELEN Oh. I see . . .

TOM I was going to tell you, but then we just got to talking, is all.

HELEN Right. (*Beat.*) He seems okay. Nice. And he works with you?

TOM Uh-huh. Down the hall. I mean, not *with* me, but . . . I see him around.

HELEN Got it. (*Beat.*) . . . Did I mention my second interview that I got? It's for that . . . I did, didn't I? Yeah.

They both return to eating their meals. Silence. A long one, in fact. Finally, TOM *stops and looks at* HELEN.

TOM I know that you know. I mean, I can tell. That you do. I made a . . . he thinks that this is, like, a *business* dinner, and I didn't say anything. So, I want you to know that I'm sorry. I am. He really just surprised me and I got all . . . I did wanna say something, but . . . I didn't.

HELEN It's okay. It's something to work on, then, right?

TOM Yep. That's true.

They both take another bite or two of their food. After a moment, TOM *reaches over and gives* HELEN *a kiss on the mouth. She responds, and the moment grows in intensity.*

"Getting Back to Business"

TOM *at his desk, working.* CARTER *sprawled on a couch and reading a magazine. He holds up a photo for* TOM *to look at. They both smile.*

After a moment, JEANNIE *appears in the doorway. Silent but staring over at* TOM. CARTER *notices her first.*

CARTER Hi, Jeannie. What's up?

JEANNIE Hey. (*to* CARTER) Gee, you're in here and not working. That comes as quite a shock . . .

CARTER Yeah, it's my gift.

JEANNIE No kidding.

JEANNIE *is done with* CARTER *and turns to* TOM. *Stares.*

TOM *What?* Good morning, by the way . . .

JEANNIE Good morning, Tom. How's things?

TOM You know. Okay.

JEANNIE I'll bet. I will just bet. (*Beat.*) Carter, can you give us a minute, please?

CARTER Not if this is gonna get good . . . (*to* TOM) Do you want me to go?

JEANNIE Please . . .

TOM I don't . . . I'm not afraid of us talking in front of him. He'll find out, anyway.

CARTER Exactly! I promise not to say a word.

JEANNIE Yeah, just print a story in the *newsletter* . . .

CARTER Well, I gotta get it out somehow.

CARTER *laughs, but no one joins in. He sputters out and sits back.*

JEANNIE Fine. Whatever.

TOM Seriously . . . Jeannie, if you wanna say something to me, go ahead. (*He stands up.*) That's fine.

JEANNIE Then why're you standing?

TOM What? Oh, you know, just . . . I felt like stretching.

CARTER *laughs.* JEANNIE *glances over at him—he smiles and mimes zipping his mouth shut. She turns back to* TOM.

JEANNIE You know I'm in accounting, right? You do know that.

TOM Of course.

JEANNIE So anything you turn in is going to come past me, I mean, over my desk. True?

TOM I guess . . .

JEANNIE No, you *know* it. I know that you know because I've had you come in there, to my office, looking for stuff before. An old receipt or some stack of files. I mean, it's how we first . . .

TOM No, you're right. That's true. . . .

JEANNIE We *met* that way, so I'm sure you realize the way these things go. The course they take. You turn in your expense reports, attach the receipts, and write in the little explanations, and we do the rest. You know all this.

TOM Yeah, Jeannie, I get it. I mean, I know how to do that. So . . . ?

JEANNIE I waited for the Chicago dinner to come through, just so I could see. I heard Carter joking around about it, and so I wanted to, you know, check out who you were with. (*Beat.*) But nothing has been turned in yet. Why's that? Because you've always been—how can I put this?—pretty damn *anal* about it before.

TOM, *glancing over at* CARTER, *doesn't say anything.*

CARTER One quick interjection? This is not my fault here. It was just an offhanded comment, that's all.

JEANNIE Just shut up, okay?

CARTER I'm done.

JEANNIE Good. (*Turns.*) Tom? What's up?

TOM *Nothing.* Jesus, I mean . . .

JEANNIE I'm just curious. But it's also my business, so, you know . . .

TOM What, to, like, *stalk* me?

JEANNIE Please, you *wish* . . . To keep up on how people are utilizing their expense accounts, shit like that.

TOM So, what? You're busting me for *not* asking to be reimbursed?

JEANNIE No . . . I'm keeping things straight. All right? It's my *job*.

TOM Yeah, but I bet you're not . . . you know, down at everybody's office, going through all their . . .

JEANNIE Yeah, I do, as a matter of fact. I stay here late almost every night, digging through mountains of crap that you guys spend out there on the road and in restaurants and at your little luxury hotels, so it's not just you. All right? Please do not flatter yourself . . .

TOM Whatever.

JEANNIE Yeah, "whatever." That's exactly what I'm asking. "Hey, 'whatever' happened to that Chicago dinner that Tom supposedly went on?"

JEANNIE *finishes and waits.* CARTER *sits up, interested.*

TOM I . . . I guess I must've forgot.

JEANNIE To what?

TOM To turn in the report. My receipts and stuff. I'll . . . I can staple it to next month's, right?

JEANNIE You could. Or I can take it from you now, if you want.

TOM No, I'm . . . I've got it all back at my apartment, so . . . later's fine.

JEANNIE It was a business dinner, right? With the guys from Chicago.

TOM Yes.

CARTER It's what he told me. (*Holds up a hand.*) Sorry . . .

TOM I mean, not with the "guys," per se, but this woman. One woman who came in from . . . yeah. A woman.

CARTER Helen, I think. (*Looks at* TOM.) *What?* I'm just being helpful . . .

TOM Yeah, thanks. (*to* JEANNIE) She was in town, and we sat down and had a meal and talked over the, I mean, some of the . . . accounts from there. Like Amtel and . . . others.

JEANNIE I see. Fine.

TOM All right? Can we put the *hot tongs* away now, or was there some more stuff that you wanted to . . . ?

TOM *tries to laugh, and* CARTER *joins in.* JEANNIE *stares.*

JEANNIE Carter, can you please leave us alone for a second? *Please.*

CARTER But . . . this is fun. Tom?

TOM No, Jeannie, shit . . . this is my office and he can . . . *what* is up with you?!

JEANNIE God, fine. Whatever you want. . . . you scared or something?

TOM Ummmm . . . maybe. Yeah. I wouldn't exactly want you handling a Ginsu knife right now or anything. . . .

CARTER *laughs again, which makes* TOM *giggle a bit.*

JEANNIE Chicago doesn't have a record of anybody coming here last month. No one. No employee—man, woman. *Fat chick.* Nothing. I verified.

TOM You called Chicago?

JEANNIE I did, yes.

TOM Jeannie, I mean, shit . . . that is . . . that's, like, so . . .

JEANNIE . . . within my *job* description.

TOM No, that goes beyond your . . . I mean, let's be honest here, you are . . . being a little nuts about this!

JEANNIE If I am, you made me that way.

TOM I didn't do . . . (*to* CARTER) Dude, back me up here.

CARTER *starts to speak, but* JEANNIE *cuts him off.*

JEANNIE And so I found it odd—especially when I had to maneuver around the *girth* issue, trying to describe her from what Carter had said—and I'm just drawing blanks from this woman over the phone who's probably thinking I'm some crazy person, but I have all the right information and the clearances, and so she's accessing a bunch of these personnel records but, uh-uh, nothing. Not a single flight booked here in over two months. *So* . . . I slapped one of those little Post-it flags on it and came down here to ask you about the thing. Maybe you can help me out.

TOM *looks over at* CARTER, *who holds up a finger.*

CARTER I never said "fat."

JEANNIE Carter, you told me she was huge.

CARTER Yeah . . . which is totally different. Shaq is huge, but nobody says the guy's fat . . .

JEANNIE You said she was a *pig*!

CARTER I don't think we should get off on a tangent here . . . (*to* TOM) I mean, Tom, you're the one who said she was in from Chicago.

TOM No . . .

CARTER You didn't?

TOM No, I was . . . you inferred that . . .

CARTER Yeah, because you told me you were having dinner with the . . . so, was she or not?

JEANNIE That's really the question, isn't it? (*Beat.*) Tom.

TOM She was . . . yes, I was having dinner with one of our, she's a colleague from Chicago, but from one of our subsidiary suppliers . . . I should've been clear about the . . . her . . .

CARTER The name was Helen, I believe.

TOM Right, Helen. About Helen's trip to . . . to see us. About the . . . stuff.

JEANNIE Tom, listen to yourself. Stop. You are, like, the worst liar ever. I mean it. In *history*.

TOM Fine. Whatever you say.

TOM *sits again, frustrated.* JEANNIE *approaches* TOM.

TOM *What?*

JEANNIE Ummm . . . just the obvious stuff. Who-was-it?

TOM She's a . . . just this girl.

JEANNIE A "girl."

TOM Woman, then! I dunno. You know I mean "woman." A woman I met. She's someone that I've . . . who I took out once, just got talking to at lunch one time and I was . . . yeah.

JEANNIE *is lost for words.* CARTER *is connecting the dots.*

JEANNIE I see. And, so, she's . . . ?

CARTER Oh . . . shit. Fuck! Are you fucking kidding me?! HOLY SHIT!!

CARTER *realizes he is being loud and gets up, crosses to the door, and shuts it. Smiling broadly.*

CARTER Dude . . . This is not her. You gotta tell me, tell me that much. This is not the . . . *her* her. Is it?

TOM Yeah. (*Beat.*) *Yes*, Carter.

CARTER Oh-my-God. Oh-my—

TOM Just stop, okay?

Fat Pig　　　　　　　　　　　　　　　　　　　　　　　　45

CARTER I mean . . . OH-MY-GOD! This is a . . . Jesus Christ!! She's—

TOM Would you just get out of here?! I mean it. Both of you . . .

JEANNIE Fine, Tom, I'll go.

CARTER Yeah, I gotta go find my camera . . . "Tommy Joins the Circus!"

TOM Asshole.

CARTER Oh, come on, man! You'd be doing the same thing to me . . .

TOM Bullshit . . .

CARTER That's a lie, and you know it! You *totally* would . . .

TOM No, I wouldn't. Nope. (*Beat.*) We mess around a lot, but I do not make fun of your . . . you know . . .

JEANNIE So . . . you are seeing her, then.

TOM It's not, no, but why do I have to discuss this?! We're on the clock here. Come on . . .

JEANNIE Sure, fine, but if you wanna stop and talk about the *Celtics* for two hours with the guys, that'd be okay, right? Yeah, that's cool . . . But if I come in here because I'm trying to figure out just what the hell is going on in my relationship, well, that's something we better talk about later. Let's save that for some *later* time. Yeah, that's pretty fair!

TOM We don't *have* a relationship!!

JEANNIE Oh, really?!

TOM No, we don't . . . I'm sorry, but you keep saying that, and I'm . . . you know . . . I keep trying to tell you that I'm not, this isn't . . .

JEANNIE You said you wanted to try again! YOU told me that!!

TOM To keep you from nagging at me!! Just to stop you from

calling and going on and on and *on* about this all the time!!
That's why!!!

JEANNIE Oh.

TOM Okay? I mean, God . . .

JEANNIE I see.

TOM I'm sorry, but . . . I just don't . . .

JEANNIE Then fine. Good.

JEANNIE suddenly reaches across the desk and smacks TOM *across the face. Hard, with an open palm. He stumbles back and hits his chair, which rolls out from under him.*

JEANNIE walks to the door, swings it open wide. Before she goes, however, she turns back to CARTER *and pushes him hard against the couch.* JEANNIE *exits, slamming the door behind her.*

TOM crosses to the door, opens it. Looks out. Holds up a hand to someone down the hall. Closes the door again.

CARTER I think she took that pretty well.

TOM You dick.

CARTER Hey, don't blame this shit on me.

TOM I'm not, I just . . . damn it! Why do we even have to do this crap? Get all involved with people and . . . ?

CARTER Because . . . we're clingy. It's what makes us different than the rest of the animals.

TOM Yeah, thanks, that really helps.

CARTER I do what I can . . .

TOM sits back down in his chair, and CARTER *plops back on the couch. They sit in silence for a moment.*

CARTER Hey . . .

TOM What?

CARTER This isn't meant as a . . . you know, to make up for what I said or whatnot, but . . . my mom was fat. *Is.*

TOM That's *great*.

CARTER No, I'm just saying . . . I know what it's like, I mean, why you were so embarrassed or . . .

TOM I wasn't, I just . . . hell. I dunno. I sorta froze and, and then . . . .

CARTER Dude, I understand. Like, totally. (*Beat.*) I used to walk ahead of her in the mall or, you know, not tell her about stuff at school so there wouldn't be, whatever. My own *mom*. I mean . . . I'm fifteen and worried about every little thing, and I've got this fucking *sumo wrestler* in a housecoat trailing around behind me. That's about as bad as it can get! I'm not kidding you. And the thing was, I blamed her for it. I mean, it wasn't a disease or like some people have, thyroid or that type of deal . . . she just shoveled shit into her mouth all the time, had a few kids, and, bang, she's up there at 350, maybe more. It used to seriously piss me off. My dad was always working late . . . golfing on weekends, and I knew it was because of her. It had to be! How's he gonna love something that looks like that, get all sexy with her? I'm just a kid at the time, but I can remember thinking that.

TOM God, that's . . .

CARTER Yeah, it's whatever, but . . . this once, in the grocery store, we're at an Albertsons and pushing *four* baskets around—you wanna know how humiliating that shit is?—and I'm supposed to be at a game by seven, I'm on JV, and she's just farting around in the candy aisle, picking up bags of "fun-size" Snickers and checking out the *calories*. Yeah. I

48   Neil LaBute

mean, what is that?! So, I suddenly go off on her, like, this sophomore in high school, but I'm all screaming in her face . . . "Don't look at the package, take a look in the fucking *mirror*, you cow!! PUT 'EM DOWN!" Holy shit, there's stock boys—bunch of guys I know, even—are running down the aisle. Manager stumbling out of his glass booth there, the works. (*Beat.*) But you know what? She doesn't say a word about it. Ever. Not about the swearing, the things I called her, nothing. Just this, like, one tear I see . . . as we're sitting at a stoplight on the way home. That's all.

TOM Wow. I'm, I mean . . .

CARTER I did feel that way, though. Maybe I shouldn't've yelled or . . . but it was true, what I said. You don't like being fat, there's a pretty easy remedy, most times. Do-not-jam-so-much-food-in-your-fucking-gullet. (*Beat.*) It's not that hard.

TOM Right. I guess that's true. (*Beat.*) It's confusing, though, the . . .

CARTER What?

TOM I dunno, I'm, like . . . I mean, that night, when you saw us? Why didn't I just come clean, say that I was having dinner, out with a friend even, instead of making all that shit up?

CARTER Because you're a pussy.

TOM Man, come on . . .

CARTER No, I say that in the best way. We all are—guys, I mean—if it comes right down to it. Very rare is the dude who stands up for the shit he believes in . . .

TOM I know! I wanna be better at that sorta stuff, but a lot of the time I'm just . . . yeah. A big wuss and I hate that! Despise that about me, but God, it's . . . No. I'm gonna work on it, I'll . . . I'll . . .

CARTER Dude, relax, take a breath, don't hurt yourself . . . We can't all be Thomas More. And anyway, look what happened to him! Poor bastard . . .

TOM True. (*Beat.*) No offense, but how the hell do *you* know about Thomas More?

CARTER Hey . . . I only cheated off the top *two* percentile in my class.

TOM *nods and drifts.* CARTER *does the same. Silence.*

TOM Geez, I wish Jeannie wasn't so, you know. Damn.

CARTER She's pissed. I mean, nobody likes getting screwed around . . .

TOM I didn't . . . (*Beat.*) You think this is how I wanted it to end up? Huh?

CARTER No . . . but it's the way these things usually do.

TOM I guess.

CARTER I *know.* The guy who first thought up the whole "I hope we can still be friends" thing must be giggling his dick off somewhere . . .

TOM Probably. (*Beat.*) You think maybe I should go down there and talk to her? Just . . .

CARTER Oh, yeah, that's a good idea. Meet her on her turf . . . with all those accounting chicks around. *Perfect.*

TOM I don't want her all mad, though. Maybe just an e-mail . . .

CARTER Yeah, with one of those smiley-face icons or something. Come on, be serious!

TOM What?

CARTER It's over. You are so done . . .

TOM I *know.* I'm not saying to try and salvage anything but just so that we can . . . shit, I dunno! We have to work together, so . . .

CARTER It's the way of the world. Breakups are ugly. I mean, unless you get to watch 'em from over here. (*Laughs.*) She so nailed you!

TOM Come on, Carter, don't.

CARTER I'm sorry, but it was awesome. I mean, I've seen you get tagged by some bad boys playing ball, never even budge—and this little girl walks in and takes you out like *Sonny Liston* . . . BAM!! Pretty cool.

TOM Yeah, hilarious. (*Beat.*) Maybe I'll just send her a quick one . . .

CARTER *waves him off and picks up another magazine.* TOM *quickly types something on his computer and hits a button to send it off.*

TOM It can't hurt.

CARTER Not as much as your cheek, anyway.

They sit and stare at each other for a moment. Silence.

CARTER You got a photo? Of her.

TOM You are not getting a picture. Not even a peek . . .

CARTER I will not take it. I promise.

TOM Uh-huh. Sure.

CARTER I won't! I just wanna see her one more time.

TOM Man, you are so . . . I don't even get why I like you.

CARTER Because you're *like* me.

TOM No, I'm not.

CARTER You so are! Absolutely.

TOM That's not true. (*Grins.*) No.

CARTER *Right.* (*Beat.*) You do that little-boy thing, the "I'm so innocent" trick that women eat up, but you are so much like me it's not even funny. Seriously . . .

TOM Carter, that's not at all . . .

CARTER Bullshit! You laugh at the same jokes and check out the same asses that I do, you date all these gals and act like you're Mr. Sensitive, but how does it always end up? The *exact* same way it does for me . . . you get bored or cornered or feel a touch nervous, and you drop 'em like they were *old produce*. Every time. Dude, I'm not blind . . .

TOM Yeah, but that's because . . . I mean, with Jeannie it's been . . . you know.

CARTER I'm not talking about her. I mean with anybody. Since I've known you. There's no shame in it . . . it's not very nice, but I don't think we were put down here to be nice. Not exclusively, anyway. Every so often we sprinkle a little "nice" on top, just to keep 'em guessing, but . . . that's about it.

TOM You scare me a little . . . I mean it.

CARTER Ahh, it's just Tuesday. Tuesdays suck . . .

They stretch out and contemplate this for a bit. CARTER *yawns and turns back to his friend.*

CARTER Seriously . . . can I see her?

TOM No.

CARTER Tom, that's not very . . . I said some stuff, and I'm sorry. I didn't know you two were dating.

TOM We're *not*. I just took her out a few . . . she's nice. Okay?

CARTER It's fine. (*Beat.*) So, lemme see.

TOM Jesus . . . (*Pulls a snapshot out of his wallet.*) I'm holding it.

CARTER That's mature. (*Goes over to look at it.*) Oh, cool. It's one of those "glamour shots," isn't it?

TOM I guess. Yes.

CARTER Very nice. I like the *boa*.

TOM Don't be a prick, or I'm gonna—

CARTER Kidding! She's sweet. I mean, from meeting her and everything, I could tell.

TOM Thanks.

CARTER Does she . . . I mean, does her weight go up and down or . . . ? I only ask because she's got a nice face, so I'm curious.

TOM She's not all worried about that kind of thing, buying into all those dietary fads. Which is sort of refreshing, actually . . .

CARTER Sure. I'm just saying . . . can't turn on CNN without some doctor . . .

TOM Because, you know . . . yeah, I think she's pretty as well, but we don't ever talk about that. "What if?" kinds of shit. She's happy with who she is, and so . . . it's . . .

CARTER Then great. (*Looks again.*) Can you please let me . . . I'm not *six* years old. I promise not to take it.

TOM 'Kay.

TOM *very warily lets go of the photo. In stages. Finally, it is in* CARTER's *hands. He studies it.*

CARTER No, I can tell that she's a very genuine person, even from a photo. I like the sunburst effect in the background. (*Smiles.*) That's a *joke.*

TOM Here, just give it back.

CARTER Wait . . . I'm serious, though, if she lost, like, eighty

pounds, she'd be kinda stunning. Could probably get on one
of those *reality* shows.

TOM I know, but I just said . . . here.

CARTER I mean, I'm only talking. I'm not an expert. Perhaps we
should see what everybody in the *cafeteria* thinks . . .

TOM Carter! CARTER, YOU FUCKER!!

But TOM *is trapped behind his desk, and* CARTER *is off like a
rocket—out the door and down the hall.* TOM *starts to follow
but gives up after a second. Returns to his desk.*

TOM Bastard. Ahh, screw it. I don't care. I'm not gonna be . . .
whatever.

A little bell goes off. Ding! TOM *looks at his computer and sees
an e-mail has arrived. He clicks it and reads.*

TOM "FUK U AND UR FAT BITCH. ASSHOLE. LOL." (*Beat.*)
That's *charming* . . .

TOM *starts to type a response, but it slowly dissolves as he
begins to pound harder and harder on the keys. Finally, he
stops, exhausted. Pushes the keyboard away. Sits.*

"Old Territory for the New Couple"

A bedroom. TOM *and* HELEN *are lying on top of the covers,*
*watching a movie—*HELEN *is concentrating,* TOM *is kissing*
her.

TOM . . . mmmmmmm. God, you're so . . .

TOM *continues to kiss her as* HELEN *watches the TV.*

HELEN Tom . . . hold on . . . look. . .

TOM I am. At *you* . . .

HELEN Remember this part? (*pointing*) I think he's just about to
. . . they're gonna find the gold . . .

Sound of gunfire, shouts. HELEN *laughs.* TOM *looks at her.*

TOM Pretty *funny.* He got shot.

HELEN Yeah, but it's meant to be . . . you know. It's a comedy.
Mostly.

TOM Uh-huh. (*Kisses her.*) Mmmmmm . . .

HELEN Wait . . .

TOM I don't wanna *wait* . . . I wanna . . . well, *lots* of things.
Kiss you. And . . . more kisses, or . . .

HELEN But . . . this is due back tomorrow.

TOM Oh, *okay* . . . (*Laughs.*) I love your mouth. Each lip. Both.

HELEN Thank you. (*kissing him*) Thanks.

TOM I really do like the way you kiss. So much.

HELEN You too. I mean, I like it. *Love* it . . . I do. We fit, you know? Our mouths together. It's important.

TOM I, yeah . . . agree . . .

HELEN *and* TOM *begin to make out—the movie is forgotten. He reaches around, finds the remote, and the sound drops out. After a moment, she gently pulls back, studies him.*

HELEN So, you feel comfortable with me? I mean . . .

TOM I'm . . . yes. I am. I have honestly never been more relaxed around a person. (*Beat.*) Well, my *mother*, but that gets into a weird area . . .

HELEN Ha-ha-ha. (*Beat.*) . . . I'm trying to seem so cool but I'm dying inside. You make me feel all . . . *everything.*

TOM Seriously, I haven't felt this way for a long time. *Ever*, probably.

HELEN I'm glad.

TOM I mean it. (*Beat.*) . . . I staggered into some pretty shitty relationships in the last few years, I mean, a couple real stinkers. (*Beat.*) . . . This is completely different. With you.

HELEN Tom, listen, I have faith in you. *Total.* I do . . .

TOM I know, I see that, and it makes me feel great. (*Beat.*) I just want you to know, though, to see how much it means to me, being with you . . . (*Kisses her.*) I *adore* you.

HELEN Thank you. Thanks. Me, too. (*She kisses him.*) And I wasn't trying to get that out of you . . .

TOM Right, I know. I just wanted to be as up front as possible . . . I had a bad streak. With women. A *certain* kind of woman . . .

HELEN Okay. (*Beat.*) Me, too. I mean, with relationships. Not women . . .

TOM Oh . . . damn! I was gonna ask if you had any *friends* who might want to join us or . . .

HELEN *punches him playfully on the shoulder, which leads to horseplay. After a moment,* TOM *lies back. Relaxed.*

TOM God, this feels so damn good! You know? I mean . . . just lying around here, us together. All alone.

HELEN I know.

TOM It's like . . . I feel like we're on a raft or something. Paddling along, all the time in the world . . . no one around to bug us. (*Mimes paddling.*) Ahhh, this is the life!

HELEN Like the beginning of *Heaven Knows, Mr. Allison.* Remember?

TOM Exactly! Yep . . . (*Smiles.*) And you could play the Deborah Kerr part. You'd make a very *saucy* nun . . .

HELEN *kisses him, and* TOM *slips back into a comfortable position.*

HELEN Sounds good. (*Beat.*) Sorta.

TOM What?

HELEN I dunno, I just . . . I do feel something. A kind of isolated. At times.

TOM Helen . . . haven't I been with you every day? I mean, my friends have even said things. Noticed it. I'm hardly with them anymore.

HELEN But . . . that's what I mean.

TOM What?

HELEN Neither am I. You know? I mean, we've been going out for, like . . . however long, and I only met that one guy. Carter. At the restaurant.

TOM That's true, but . . . I mean, I've been waiting for the, maybe, a right time or something. One of those office parties or . . .

HELEN Tom.

TOM No, truthfully. I thought maybe on the Fourth or . . . we do a big party at the beach. A cookout and stuff.

HELEN Great . . . should I go with a *thong*, or be a little more conventional?

TOM Very funny. I was being serious . . .

A sort of silence drops over them. Both of them stare off, quiet.

HELEN It's just a little like we're, I dunno, hiding or whatever. From people.

TOM No . . .

HELEN You don't think?

TOM No, Helen, I really don't. At all. (*Beat.*) I mean, we're not exactly hanging out with all your pals, either. We've barely . . .

HELEN That's not true. I ask you all the time if you'd want to, or if we . . .

TOM Yeah, but . . .

HELEN I'm dying to show you off, Tom, if you'd let me . . . I've told you to pick me up at work, all kinds of things!

TOM I know, but . . . it's a *library*. Not supposed to talk in there . . .

HELEN Tom . . . *please*. (*She waits.*) Listen, I had a thing come up for me at the . . . this opportunity. Remember the interview that I . . . yeah. That. It's a couple towns over, but far enough away that . . . whatever. The *point* is, it's a great offer and the more I think about this—every time we end up in the back of a café or slipping into a movie late, after it's already going—some little thing in my head, this warning buzzer says, "Watch it. Just watch out."

TOM Helen . . .

HELEN I just hope you're not *embarrassed* by me in some way, because, well I mean . . . I don't know what . . .

TOM No. Why would you say that? I'm not at all . . . What're you . . . ?

HELEN Nothing. I'm not saying anything, except I need you to be honest with me here. *Today*, if possible.

TOM Well, what am I supposed to say now? To that?

HELEN Just the truth.

TOM I'm . . . I meant something easier.

HELEN *smiles at this as* TOM *scoots closer to her on the bed, holds her. A kiss.*

TOM Helen . . . you can't leave town, I need you around. You're like the sunrise to me. Like vitamin C or something. My *oxygen.* (*Beat.*) I need you . . .

HELEN I'm not looking for fairy-tale or out-of-the-ballpark or anything . . . just a person who cares about me like I do him. Simple.

TOM . . . Love isn't simple. It's . . . *never having to say you're sorry.*

TOM *starts to say more, but* HELEN *stops him. Smiles.*

HELEN I don't need you to be clever here! No jokes. Or *film quotes* . . . Just be very clear . . . and honest.

TOM *kisses* HELEN, *then* *sits her down on the bed. Joins her. Tries to get serious.*

TOM Fine. Look . . . I wanna be truthful now, so just let me . . . you know, bumble along. All right?

HELEN Please. Bumble on.

She smiles, and TOM *slowly returns it to her. He touches her face. Strokes her hair.*

TOM Helen . . . I want you. Both mentally *and* physically. Each curve, every last inch of you . . . (*He kisses her.*) I'd hope you can see that by now . . .

She starts to speak, but he holds up a finger to silence her.

TOM So . . . I don't know how to do this. To say exactly how I'm feeling because, you know, I'm a guy, and we're taught how to *kick* stuff and tear the wings off shit—but, look . . . I can see that we've got something here, I'm not stupid, right?—do not answer that—and I need you to know. That *I* know. I'm really just so damn . . . *overcome* by this. Here. Us. I don't take it lightly or in some carefree manner at all. No. Helen, you are just, well, very important to me . . . *very* . . . (*Beat.*) Look, I'm falling for you, falling *hard*, and . . . yeah. I am, and I hope that you give me a chance to prove that in the near future, at the, aforementioned volleyball-slash-beach party or at some other to-be-determined public gathering. (*Beat.*) And if you take that other job, even a few towns over, it'd be a real, you know. Bad thing. (*Grins.*) Okay, that sort've sucked, but most of the ingredients were in there . . .

HELEN Yeah . . . and it was kind of lovely.

TOM Then, good. Thanks.

HELEN No, thank you . . . Tom Sullivan.

TOM You're welcome . . . Helen . . . what's your last name again?

HELEN *smacks him playfully on the shoulder. Twice.*

TOM I know it has, like, a "B" in it.

HELEN Bond. (*Laughs.*) You ass . . .

TOM Right, Bond, sorry. Bond. (*Kisses her.*) You're awesome.

HELEN You, too, Tom. You're a good man. (*Kisses him back.*) Good and strong and brave and . . . ummmm . . . *lots* of nice things . . .

TOM . . . mmmmmm. I love it when you talk *dirty.*

TOM *begins to kiss her. More and more.* HELEN *responds and, after a moment, lets him unfasten her bra.* TOM *starts to caress and kiss her there.* HELEN's *eyes slowly close.*

Her hand searches around, finds the remote again. Click! Up come the sounds of war and mayhem on the soundtrack. Loud.

"Twists and Turns at the Office"

TOM *at his desk again. Working.* JEANNIE *standing nearby with a file in her hand. Waiting.*

JEANNIE . . . So are you bringing her to the thing next
   month?

TOM Huh? (*Looks up.*) Oh, yeah. I think.

JEANNIE Not sure?

TOM Ummm, you know . . . she's gotta check if she can get off
   from work.

JEANNIE Oh. I see. And what's she do?

TOM She's a . . . printed-word specialist.

JEANNIE Ahh. (*to herself*) Perfect.

TOM What's that?

JEANNIE Nothing. (*Points.*) Are you almost done there? I need
   to get those out by five . . .

TOM Yeah, hold on.

TOM *goes back to work while* JEANNIE *glances around. Takes in the space.*

JEANNIE No pictures of her up yet.

TOM Nah.

JEANNIE How come?

TOM, *frustrated, drops his pen and looks straight at her.*

TOM Wasn't the one that appeared on everybody's *desktop* this morning enough? (*Turns his monitor around.*) You need more laughs than this?

JEANNIE I wouldn't mind.

TOM Great.

JEANNIE Yeah, I'd be up for that.

TOM Jesus . . . you really are awful, you know that? I mean it.

JEANNIE Just keep signing, okay? Your little sermon isn't necessary.

TOM I'm not . . . whatever.

JEANNIE That's exactly right. What-ever.

TOM Jeannie . . . can't we just be . . . ?

JEANNIE Don't bother. *Sign.*

TOM *is about to follow instructions but pulls the files from the desk and slips them in a drawer. Shuts it. Sits back as he checks his watch.*

TOM No, uh-uh, you've got time. And I want you to tell me . . . Go on. What the hell I did to you that was so bad. Do it.

JEANNIE Tom, don't be a prick, all right? I need to make FedEx.

TOM You will, just—

JEANNIE No! I'm not obligated to talk with you about shit . . . We're co-workers, we *work* together now, and that is all. Give me the files.

TOM Nope.

JEANNIE You're an asshole . . .

TOM Maybe so. I dunno . . . maybe I am. Or have been to you.

That's what I'm saying! If I have, then tell me. Show me
how . . .

It's a standoff for a moment, then JEANNIE *makes a move toward*
TOM. *He stands up and holds his ground. She backs off and*
retreats to one side, hands on her hips.

JEANNIE I don't even wanna discuss your fat bitch, okay?
   She's—
TOM Stop that.
JEANNIE So, forget it. I'll just say about us, I mean, what
   we've . . .
TOM No, let's do the whole . . .
JEANNIE Fuck you! Don't tell me what we'll do. At all.
TOM I'm *not*. I'm just saying we should probably, you
   know . . .
JEANNIE We should've *probably* done a lot of things! We should
   probably be engaged now, if you weren't such a spineless
   shit, like every other guy. So . . .
TOM Your mouth is, like, I dunno. Wow.
JEANNIE Yeah, exactly right. "Wow." I'm twenty-eight years old,
   and I just keep hitting the booby prize, and you know what?
   After a while, it really starts to get you down . . .
TOM But, I'm not . . . that's not my . . .
JEANNIE Problem? I didn't say that. It's no one's problem, *me*
   included . . . it just sucks. That's what I'm saying. (*Beat.*) I
   thought maybe you were different, but you ended up being
   the same kind of lame guy that I perpetually date, and it just
   freaks me out a little. That maybe you're the only type out
   there. These baby boys who run around in nice clothes, but

all they really wanna do is *breast-feed* for the rest of their days . . .

TOM I don't . . . I can't speak for other people, Jeannie, but I—

JEANNIE I don't care anymore. I don't.

TOM I'm just saying that . . . you and I didn't end up working out, but it doesn't mean . . . I like you. I did always *like* you, but . . . we're . . .

JEANNIE Tom, I know you think that means something to me, but it's really just drivel. Okay? More of the same.

TOM Fine. I'm sorry.

JEANNIE And that doesn't do shit, either.

TOM *nods, then sits and pulls out the files. Signs his name in several more places and then holds them out.* JEANNIE *goes over and grabs them. Hovers.*

TOM Yes?

JEANNIE I know I said I wasn't gonna . . . but I really need to know.

TOM What?

JEANNIE Her. (*Points at computer screen.*) What's the story with that one?

TOM Jeannie . . .

JEANNIE I mean, I hope it's some mothering thing or whatever, because if not, it's just so off-the-charts gross that I don't know what to say.

TOM We should probably stop now.

JEANNIE I mean, you know what everybody is saying around here, right? I know that you know. And it doesn't even faze you, huh? At all?

TOM I'm . . . I don't wanna do this. Here.

JEANNIE It's not like she's . . . She's really *fat*, Tom! A fat sow
and you know it. I can tell you're aware by the way you're
acting, which is really the puzzling part . . .

TOM I-like-her. *End* of story.

JEANNIE Yeah, but what the hell? Did you do something bad in
some other life that you're making up for? Tell me, because
she's . . . well, you know what she's like better than the rest
of us . . . I mean . . . is she a good *cook*, or . . . ?

TOM STOP IT! Jeannie, just stop this. I get that you're pissed at
me and you needed to blow off some steam, so that's why I,
I . . . I allowed you to say stuff, but . . .

JEANNIE You didn't "allow" me shit, Tom! I can say whatever I
want, *any*time I want. The whole company is, why should *I*
be any different?

TOM Then talk if you want to! I-DO-NOT-CARE!!! I enjoy her
because she's not you, *anything* like you . . . she's not
obsessed with looks and money and clothes and useless
bullshit like that! OKAY?! (*Beat.*) I like who I am when I'm
with her, okay, so just . . . fuck, just leave us alone . . .

JEANNIE Ohhhh . . . "us." So it's "*us*" now, huh?

TOM Yeah. It is.

JEANNIE And, forgive me for saying it, but she seems a little
obsessed with some things . . . like maybe *Cheetos*.

TOM *starts to come around his desk now, determined to put an
end to this.* JEANNIE *stares him down.*

TOM I'm serious here . . . you need to go.

JEANNIE I am going, I *am*, but not because you say so. Because
I want to. I want to be as far away from you as I can be . . .

TOM Good.

JEANNIE Yeah, "good." Nice *retort*.

TOM Just . . .

JEANNIE What an *ass*. (*Beat*.) I'm sure you thought this would hurt me, right? Like, "What's the worst thing I'd be able to do to her?" And this is what you came up with, some self-image killer like this one . . . Tom ditched me for fucking *Mama Cass*! Boo-hoo, woe is me! She's fat, so does that mean that Tom secretly digs fat chicks, does it mean that *I'm* fat?! Huh?!! Is that what all this *shit* is about, getting back at me?!!

TOM Jeannie, get out of here! NOW!!

JEANNIE It doesn't hurt me at all! NOT ONE BIT!! It just makes you look like some creepy fucker and a totally odd . . . AHHHHHH!!! I don't care. I hate you. HATE-YOU. So, so much.

JEANNIE *storms out of his office, leaving the door wide open.* TOM *doesn't have the strength to close it; he crosses to his couch instead and sits. Rubs his eyes.*

When he opens them, he sees CARTER *standing at the door.*

TOM Go away. Seriously.

CARTER That's not very neighborly.

TOM Neighbors don't treat neighbors this way. Enemies barely do . . .

CARTER Dude, it's a *joke*. (*Beat*.) Think of it as payback for forwarding everybody my e-mail about that one lady at lunch. And I *did* see the string of her tampon, by the way . . . when she crossed her legs. (*Shivers*.)

TOM I'm not kidding, Carter . . .

CARTER I thought Helen looked good blown up like that!
Several people I talked to said they were gonna keep it . . .

TOM Come on, man. Really. Just leave me alone today.

CARTER Fine.

But instead of leaving, CARTER *goes and drops into* TOM*'s chair and starts playing with it, swinging in circles and raising/lowering the seat mechanism.*

TOM If Moses had needed, like, another plague . . . I would've given him your number.

CARTER Bad day?

TOM I'm getting used to 'em.

CARTER That's why I'm here. To be, like, a *calming* influence.

TOM Great. If you're my best chance, then I'm screwed . . .

CARTER Nah. All will be fine, my friend. I promise.

TOM O-kay. (*Beat.*) I don't even need to ask you why you're here . . .

CARTER Just chillin'.

TOM Uh-huh. Figured.

The men sit in their respective spots for a bit, staring up at the ceiling. Finally, TOM *speaks.*

TOM So, lemme ask you something, then.

CARTER Shoot.

TOM And honestly now . . . just an opinion is all, so no big deal.

CARTER I'm ready.

TOM What do you actually think of her? Helen, I mean.

CARTER Ummmmm . . .

TOM Not for you or, like, scoping her out down in *Jamaica* or that type of thing . . . just as a person.

CARTER Oh. Like that.

TOM Yes.

CARTER *sits back in the chair, thinking for a moment.*

CARTER You're begging for trouble.

TOM That's . . . why do I even ask you?

CARTER No, and I'll tell you why! I will. I know that I'm not superfamiliar with her or anything, like, her *qualities*—of which there may be many . . .

TOM There are . . .

CARTER . . . and that's great. Terrific. But I'm just talking purely as an "Is this a good deal for my pal here?" thing.

TOM Fine. And?

CARTER *And* you got a long road ahead, that's all. Just being honest.

TOM Fine.

CARTER I'm not saying I don't admire you—I do, actually, 'cause I know that I couldn't do it!—but she's gonna end up a weight around your neck. Forgive the *pun* . . .

TOM You're . . . doing that strictly on a "physical" basis . . . which is—

CARTER Of course! Fuck, what else can I go on? (*Beat.*) I don't wanna come off like some *Elton John* here, but you're a good-looking guy. You're successful, bit of a player in the industry . . . I don't understand you taking God's good gifts and pissing on 'em . . .

TOM Carter . . .

CARTER Dude, you're the one who evoked a *biblical* thing
   earlier . . . so take a glance at Noah and all that flood shit!
   He didn't pair up the apes with the antelope, right? It's one
   of the many laws of nature. "Run with your own kind."

TOM That is so . . . out of whack that I'm, like, completely lost
   now . . .

CARTER Hey, it's a free country, and if this is how you really
   feel, then you are fucking Gunga Din. "Better man than I
   am" and all that shit. Just don't be surprised when you turn
   a few heads down at the mall.

TOM But why can't we . . . I mean, shit! I dunno, man, I like
   her. A *lot*. She makes me happy, and I really wanna make her
   happy, too . . .

CARTER I'm not saying she can't be happy. That she shouldn't
   meet somebody, but it oughta be a fat somebody, or a bald
   one. Whatever. Like her. A somebody that *fits* her . . .

TOM That's crazy . . . things aren't just based on *appearance*!

CARTER Maybe you should snap on the TV once in a while.
   (*Beat*.) I'm not talking about what people deserve, I'm
   saying what they *get*. You look one way, you have access to
   all this. Look some other way, all you get is that. Sorry, but
   it's true.

TOM Yeah, well, it sucks . . .

CARTER It's whatever. Truth. People are not comfortable with
   difference. You know? Fags, retards, cripples. Fat people.
   Old folks, even. They scare us or something.

TOM I don't think that's true. I mean, I'm not . . . no, Carter, I
   don't buy that. We're all . . .

CARTER Come on, be honest! The thing they represent that's so
   scary is what we *could* be, how vulnerable we all are. I
   mean, *any* of us. Some wrong gene splice, a bad backflip off

the trampoline . . . too many cartons of *Oreos*! We're all just one step away from being what frightens us. What we despise. So . . . we despise it when we see it in anybody else.

TOM Old people, though? Come *on*. We're all gonna age. It's . . .

CARTER Not me. I hope I'm a goner before then. The elderly make me sick . . .

TOM This is . . . you're not helping me, Carter! That's the most *depressing* shit I've ever heard. Seriously.

CARTER *holds up his hands and shrugs.* TOM *sits up on the couch, thinking. A bit lost.*

CARTER All I'm saying is this . . . Do what you want. If you like this girl, then don't listen to a goddamn word anybody says. Not *one*. (*Beat.*) But you've got your whole life to be a positive person, okay? To do some good in the community and be a bighearted fellow or whatever. Overlook people's flaws and plant *saplings* and shit. But you're only young once. Handsome and youthful and vibrant. So don't fuck it up, that is all I'm telling you here. Don't take a complete dump on your one moment in the sun . . . (*Beat.*) Not for somebody like her.

TOM Carter . . . you're not . . . God . . .

TOM *catches himself, stops.* CARTER *waits, bemused.*

TOM You don't always have to say something. You know? Like, *everything* that comes into your head.

Silence. After a minute, CARTER *yawns and slowly stands.*

CARTER Yeah, I should stuff an envelope or two. (*Laughs.*) So
   look . . . I wanna ask you this first, I mean, before you hear
   it from . . . I'm gonna take Jeannie to that beach deal
   coming up. Is that cool?

TOM Ummm . . . sure. No, of course.

CARTER I mean, no weirdness for us?

TOM None. I think you two could . . . just might be perfect for
   each other.

CARTER Yeah, me, too! (*Beat.*) I heard she's started going to a
   gym, so that's something.

TOM Uh-huh.

CARTER I mean, you know her body, right? Obvious potential.

TOM Course.

CARTER Anyway . . . as long as we're still . . .

TOM Sure. I think we'll remain exactly what we are. You and
   me.

CARTER Friends, right?

TOM Sorta. (*Gestures with his fingers.*) About this much . . .

CARTER Good enough for me.

CARTER *starts for the door.* TOM *gets up, and they shake hands
awkwardly. A pat on the shoulder.* CARTER *reaches into a shirt
pocket and hands* TOM *the photo of* HELEN *that he took before.*

CARTER I know you'll do the right thing.

CARTER *exits.*

TOM *crosses to his office windows and slowly closes all the blinds. One by one. The room grows darker.*

TOM *goes to the couch and lies down. Holds the picture in front of him. Brings it closer now, staring at it. Hard.*

"One of Those Blustery Beach Days"

A stretch of sand. TOM, *in a flowered swimsuit, sitting alone on a towel. Trying to focus on a biography.*

After a moment, JEANNIE *approaches. She is looking fit and is wearing a skimpy bikini. She towers over him.*

JEANNIE . . . Thought that was you.

TOM Yeah. Hey. (*Jumps up.*) You look good. I mean, *nice.*

JEANNIE Thanks. Yeah . . . I'm doing Pilates now. (*Beat.*) How come you guys are sitting way down here?

TOM Oh, we're just . . . little privacy, I suppose. Edge of the group is all.

JEANNIE Ah. Cool.

TOM So . . . (*Beat.*) You and Carter, huh?

JEANNIE Yeah, how 'bout that?!

TOM It's good.

JEANNIE I hope so. He's actually okay once you get him outta the office . . .

TOM Most people are. That's not, like, the best environment for a person. Those *cubicles* . . .

JEANNIE Probably not. (*Smiles.*) Anyways . . .

TOM Right. Anyway. I hope you guys—

JEANNIE Thanks. You, too, I guess.

JEANNIE leans toward him, and TOM *gives her a peck on the cheek.*

JEANNIE Well . . . come down and do a little volleyball later or something.

TOM Will do. Maybe.

JEANNIE 'Kay. (*Beat.*) See that you're still wearing that swimsuit I got you . . .

TOM Yes. I like it.

JEANNIE Looks good on you. (*Beat.*) All right, so I'll see you, then . . .

TOM Okay. Take care.

JEANNIE Same to you. (*Hangs on.*) And, look, about all that other stuff . . .

HELEN *arrives on the scene, juggling a large tray full of food. She is wearing a one-piece suit, a beach wrap around her waist.*

JEANNIE Hey. Get everything you need?

HELEN Yes, thanks. (*to* JEANNIE) Hello.

JEANNIE Hi, I'm Jeannie. Tom and I . . . work together.

HELEN Oh, nice. I'm Helen.

JEANNIE Yeah, I figured. (*Beat.*) I just mean, Tom mentioned you before.

HELEN Oh. (*Turns to* TOM.) That was sweet.

TOM Hey.

JEANNIE Anyhow, I came down to say hello and invite you guys over for some games later . . .

TOM Cool. We'll, ummm . . .

HELEN I'm not too sporty, but . . . not that you could tell or anything!

The two women share a little laugh. JEANNIE *glances at* TOM, *who tries to smile but only grimaces.*

TOM We'll see. Thanks, though.

HELEN Yes, we appreciate it. And really great to meet you . . .

JEANNIE You, too. So long, Tom.

TOM Okay. Bye, Jeannie . . .

JEANNIE *throws one last look at* TOM, *then heads off down the beach toward the others.* TOM *sits down on the blanket with the food.* HELEN *follows in a moment, out of breath.*

TOM So. That's Jeannie. She's in Accounting . . .

HELEN That's quite a swimsuit she's got there. For an *accountant.* (*Recovers.*) She seems nice, though.

TOM Yeah. Pretty much.

HELEN What's that mean?

TOM Oh, ya know . . . have our differences at work sometimes, that's all.

HELEN Ahh.

They settle themselves on their blanket and begin to sort the food items into two stacks.

TOM Oh, good, I'm glad they had those Kettle Chips . . . (*He looks off.*) Ahh, there's Carter.

HELEN Yeah, he said hi when I was down there.

TOM Good, that's . . . (*Yells.*) HEY, BUDDY!

HELEN You can go down there if you want.

TOM Huh? No, I wanna be here with you. We'll, you know . . . later.

HELEN 'Kay. (*looking up*) Beautiful day.

TOM Uh-huh, yep. Super nice . . .

They sit for a moment, taking in the sun. The surf.

HELEN How long do these things usually go? Any idea?

TOM Ummm, no, but . . . we don't have to stay or anything.
That's fine. I just need to, you know, make an appearance . . .

HELEN No, I like it. Being here with you and all your . . . it's
great. (*Beat.*) We just promised those guys that we'd . . . at
some point . . .

TOM Oh, right, the travel agent. Sure.

HELEN So . . . are you excited about it? The trip, I mean?

TOM Yeah. You kidding me? It's a . . . great place. I love Miami.

HELEN I sorta meant about the part where we get to be
together, but . . .

TOM Oh, that. (*Yawns.*) Yeah, that's okay.

HELEN *swats him on the arm.* TOM *reacts and sits back. She
watches him as he turns away.*

HELEN Ummm, weird vibe here, Tom. Are you sure that
you're . . .

TOM What? Of course. (*Beat.*) It's all set and everything.

HELEN That's not really the same as just saying yes.

TOM Jesus, fine . . . *yes.* Better? (*Beat.*) Food looks good.
Thanks for going down there . . .

HELEN Figured we should grab some before it was gone . . .

TOM Sorry, I should've . . .

HELEN No, it felt nice, to walk through the surf like that. Fun.

TOM Good. Glad you could make it . . .

HELEN It wasn't *that* far.

TOM No, I'm . . . I meant, switch days or whatever.

HELEN I know. Kidding. (*Beat.*) Are you?

TOM Sure, of course. Why?

HELEN I'm . . . nothing. Let's eat.

TOM No, Helen. What?

HELEN Same ol' stuff. Doesn't matter.

TOM Of course it does. Of course . . . tell me.

HELEN Look where we're at. I mean, Tom, it's . . . forget it.
   (*Holds up a hot dog.*) Ketchup?

TOM This isn't . . . Helen, I just wanted to get us near the
   dunes here, so we'd have a little protection from the wind.
   That's all.

HELEN Tom . . .

TOM I'm serious!

HELEN But we haven't . . . we didn't hardly talk to—

TOM I introduced you to people . . .

HELEN In the parking lot! As you and I were unloading stuff out
   of the car. That's not an *introduction*.

TOM Shit. I knew this would happen!

HELEN You knew it would happen because you know who you
   are, Tom. I don't think you're ready for this.

TOM Come on, I don't wanna . . . Just eat something, all right?
   We shouldn't fight.

HELEN It's not fighting, Tom. When you and I talk, that's not
   fighting. It's *talking*. That's what people do.

TOM Whatever.

HELEN *Tom* . . . what's going on?

TOM Nothing.

HELEN I told you . . . weeks ago I said to you that you needed
   to be honest. More than anything else.

TOM I know. I *know* that . . .

HELEN But you're . . . this isn't—

TOM Helen, come on, stop now! Shit . . . this is my company picnic, okay? We're supposed to be having some fun.

HELEN "Fun." Okay . . . (*She slowly stands.*) Let's go join in the big game.

HELEN *jumps up and down a few times, miming a few shots as* TOM *watches. He looks over to where his friends are.*

HELEN Come on, Tom! It's fun!!

TOM Stop it! Stop!! (*Grabs her.*) Helen, please stop that.

HELEN Fine. Then let's chat, okay? (*She sits again.*) Because it's pretty damn hard to sit out here with a smile plastered on my face . . .

TOM All right.

They sit in silence for a moment, then HELEN *reaches over and grabs a Ball Park frank. Starts to eat.*

HELEN I can't help it. I eat when I get stressed out . . .

TOM It's fine. Me, too. Sorta.

TOM *sits and watches* HELEN *eat. She slowly devours a hot dog. Bit by bit.*

TOM . . . Come on, slow down a little bit, honey . . .

HELEN Right. Okay . . . (*Beat.*) Tom, you are aware that I like you. You already know that.

TOM Yes.

HELEN But I get the feeling . . . I mean, it is now pretty obvious that there are some problems here. Issues, or whatever. And we need to get over them or . . . well, you know. Things that I don't wanna think about.

TOM I guess.

HELEN Please, you need to stay in this. Focused on it, so don't drift off or anything. I love you so much, I really do, Tom. Feel a connection with you that I haven't allowed myself to dream of, let alone be a part of, in so long. Maybe ever. But I can't be with you if you're feeling something other than that same thing that I am . . . completely and utterly open to that other person. I don't know what to say here, Tom . . . I'm worried sick. Look at me . . . when did you ever see me not eat a hot dog that was placed in front of me? Huh? (*Tries to chuckle*.) I know you hate those jokes, sorry, but I'm . . . Tom, tell me about it. I know you're thinking something, so we might as well just . . . one more thing. Just this. And I've never said this to anyone, not any other person in the world. Ever. My parents or a . . . no one. I would change for you. I would. I don't mean Slim-Fast or that one diet that the guy on TV did . . . with the sandwiches from Subway. That guy . . .

TOM Helen . . . that . . . that's not . . .

HELEN I'll do something radical to myself if you want me to. Like be stapled or have some surgery or whatever it takes— one of those *rings*—because I do not want this to end. I'm willing to do that, because of what you mean to me. The kind of, just, *ecstasy* that you've brought me. So . . . I just wanted you to know that.

TOM *sits there, taking it all in. Looking off. She nudges him with an elbow.*

HELEN This would be an excellent time to say something sweet to me. If you at all care about my feelings.

TOM I know. I'm . . . (*Beat.*) Helen, that was such a nice thing to offer.

HELEN Oh-my-God . . .

TOM What?

HELEN I just . . . the way you worded that right then, in the past tense. It scared me.

TOM No, I just . . . it *is*. Really. And I appreciate it so much.

HELEN But what? (*Beat.*) Gosh, I wish those *thousand ships* would show up right about now . . .

TOM Yeah. (*Tries to smile.*) Look, Helen . . . I've been thinking . . .

HELEN Okay.

TOM I think you are an amazing woman, I honestly do. And I really love what we have here. Our times together . . . but I think that maybe, you know, some time would be good here, or if you were to, I'm not sure . . . maybe take that job. It might tell us if we're . . . I dunno.

HELEN Oh . . . (*Beat.*) Wow, that's a bit of a . . . you know . . . I mean, why would I do that?

HELEN *tries to continue but* TOM *stops her. Waits.*

TOM Listen . . . If we were in some other time or a land that nobody else was around on . . . like that island from the movie, the Sinatra film—*None but the Brave*—then everything might be okay, I wouldn't be so fucking paranoid about what the people around me were saying. Or even thinking. Then it could just be you and me, and that'd be so great. Perfect. But . . . I guess I do care what my peers feel about me. Or how they view my choices, and yes, maybe that makes me not very deep or petty or some other word, hell, I dunno! It's my *Achilles* flaw or something. I'm . . .

TOM *stops for a moment, regrouping.* HELEN *tries to speak.*

HELEN Tom, don't do this, okay? Please don't. We can, I dunno . . . we . . .

TOM No, I need to . . . if I stop now I'm not gonna be able to . . . finish, so I'm . . . (*Beat.*) Helen . . . things are so tricky, life is. I know now I'm not really deserving of you, of all you have to offer me. I can see that now. I want to be better, to do good and better things and to make a proper sort of decision here, but I . . . I can't. I cannot do it. I mean, I could barely drive here today because of . . . my hands were shaking the whole time. They were. Jumping up and down on the wheel there. And these are all people that I know! That I . . . I'm just not gonna be able to do this, on like, a daily basis. (*Starts to cry.*) God . . . look at me! It's . . . I'm sorry about this and I wish that I was saying what you wanna hear. I do. That would make me really happy, to please another person right now. I mean, a person that I'm feeling this . . . love for. Yeah, *love*. But sometimes it just isn't enough. You know? All this love inside and it's not nearly enough to get around the shit that people *heave* at you . . . I feel like I'm drowning in it—*shit*—and I don't think I can . . . I don't wanna fight it anymore. I am just not strong enough for that, so I'm gonna lie on my back for a while and float. See if I can keep my head above the surface. (*Beat.*) I guess that's what I needed to say to you. That I'm not brave. I'm not. I know you want me to be . . . always believed that I *can* be, but I'm a weak and fearful person, Helen, and I'm not gonna get any better. Not any time soon, at least . . .

They sit quietly, not touching. TOM *is still tearful.*

HELEN But that's . . . it's something we could work on, right . . . can't we, Tom? Right?
TOM . . . No. I don't think I can.

HELEN *begins to cry.* TOM *continues to cry as well. Big, rolling tears as they both stare out to sea.*

Silence. Darkness.